Ghosts of Kilrush

Ghosts of Kilrush

By Joe Riley

As told to Alan C. Atkins

RavensYard Publishing, Ltd.

Kilrush, County Clare, Ireland / Fairfax County, Virginia USA

ISBN 1-928928-13-7

Published by
RavensYard Publishing, Ltd.
P. O. Box 176
Oakton, VA 22124 USA
www.ravensyard.com

Dedication

This book is dedicated to all of those parents who have raised or are raising children that are not biologically theirs. I want to assure them all that if they give their children even half of the love, care and affection that my own Auntie May and Uncle Andrew lavished upon me, then those children will be truly yours and yours alone. If he hasn't done so already, may God shower all of his blessings upon you.

To my town that I love so much, and the community of Kilrush, I am forever in your debt for the beauty of a childhood and memories that very few would experience. To the very special people of the town who influenced my life, I was so lucky to be exposed to their proud traditions and unselfish love. How blessed was I to be with them in such a great era, may God bless you all.

Introduction

Sunday October 15th 2002 — I had just arrived in Bellevue, near Seattle, Washington, USA for a week of meetings at the headquarters of my employer for the last 12 years— Microsoft Corporation. Those 12 years seemed like weeks for me and I realised now, at the age of 40, time can fly past you very quickly. The west coast of the United States was indeed a long way from the west coast of Ireland and a town called Kilrush, where I was born and raised.

That Sunday was like any other while away on business, an anonymous hotel room in an anonymous city. I decided around noon to check any personal email I had received over the weekend, since it would pass some time for me as I adjusted to being 8 hours out of sync with my home in Ireland.

A simple heading of "Hello" and the sender "Joe Riley" attracted my attention, since I had no idea who Joe Riley was. That it was sent on Friday 13th October went un-noticed. It began "I just had a look at your web site and the photos of home...." Joe had come across my personal website, which I have dedicated to my birthplace of Kilrush. Joe explained that he was writing a book about his childhood in Kilrush during the 1940's and 50's and he wanted to know if he could use some photos from my site which had awakened memories for him. I had made many friends around the world via that website and I was always eager to help them in what was usually a search for their roots or their past. Joe's email alas indicated he lived in the Philippines, so I was even more intrigued than usual. I immediately responded with more questions and we've not stopped talking since!

In this way I entered the odyssey of Joe Riley's "Ghosts of Kilrush". For Joe it had begun way back in 1946, when he first set foot in Kilrush at the tender age of 3. Little did he know that day that his early family life was to change forever. Here in Kilrush town was Joe Riley, a young English kid with an Irish name, a foreign accent and a Protestant to boot! Here he was in a country where Catholicism and hatred of the English were woven into the very fabric of a society that had only known political and church freedom for a couple of decades. It was still very much coming to terms with that reality.

How had he come to be there? Why was he taken from his mother at such a tender age? Why was he now writing his story some 45 years later? What had prompted him to address these ghosts?

The story that Joe unveiled to me over the following weeks was incredible. Through Joe's words I was walking the streets of my hometown with him, identifying with much of it but also seeing new and old stories from a fresh perspective. Kilrush and its people were being revealed to me through the eyes of a man not even born there! Familiar faces appeared and faces gone before my time were newly revealed to me. In the ordinary I could also see the extraordinary, from the joyful to the sorrowful. Here was a documentary of a time now past, a harsh time in many of its aspects but also a wonderful time, when uncomplicated people cared about others in a manner fast disappearing in 21st century Ireland, as in most other parts of the western world.

Joe's reason for writing the book was not just to put to

rest some ghosts of his own, but also to honour those people and ensure they would never be forgotten. This book is in honour of their memory and the author is content knowing that you are reading of the Ghosts of Kilrush.

I know you will enjoy this true story of an extraordinary childhood, set in a town that is dear to many hearts, regardless of where in the world sons and daughters of Kilrush happen to be. Reflect on its message of the power of the human spirit to overcome hardship.

Some may disagree on his recollections of specific events, but remember this is the story as a young boy saw it, from memories stored over many, many years.

This is Joe's story of his Ghosts of Kilrush........enjoy.

Pat Cusack
Native of Kilrush, County Clare, Ireland
and newfound friend of Joe Riley

CHAPTER ONE

The Dream

I don't know what it was that woke me. It may have been a bit of wind-borne debris hitting the window. Due to a typhoon passing 100 kilometres to the east of us, the wind was quite strong at that moment, but fortunately the rain was holding off. It is strange really, that we all dream at night, but rarely remember the content in the morning. If we are suddenly woken though, our dream remains vivid, as was mine at that moment. So vivid, in fact, that I knew that it was going to be hard to get back to sleep for a while. I looked at my watch. The luminous hands told me that it was just after three o'clock.

I turned to look at my wife. She lay absolutely still, her breathing was so shallow as to be almost undetectable and her lovely face was at peace. I arose slowly so as not to disturb her and walked through to the kitchen. I wanted to remember my dream, to re-live it. I took a tumbler and put in some ice cubes, then passing into the lounge, I half-filled the glass with Jameson whiskey.

I quietly unlocked the patio doors and slipped out, closing them behind me. The wind was quite strong, but pleasant. I sat in a chair facing it, letting it blow upon my face. I thought about my life, my successes and my failures.

It is strange to think about such things at a time of day

that psychiatrists have vowed that the human brain activity is at its lowest. One is not fully awake, yet one is not asleep either. It is a time when memories suppressed, maybe for many years, can at last be re-called.

My thoughts roamed through the decades of my history; the happy times, the sad times. I thought of my first wife and family from whom I had separated many years before. I felt sadness about this, for I knew that I had contributed to this break up in no small manner, but could not pinpoint the reasons for my actions.

Something deep inside me sometimes made me illogically angry, angry with life itself. I realized that it still arose to the surface occasionally; causing me to verbally lash out at those around me, even my second wife, who I loved more than life itself. I needed to find the cause.

My thoughts returned to my dream. Was my subconscious trying to tell me the reason for this anger? I knew that if I could find the problem, the solution would be easy. I thought about the dream itself. Although I could not clearly recall, I somehow knew that I had experienced the same dream many times before. My dream allowed me to revisit the happy years of my youth spent in Kilrush, County Clare in Ireland. Kilrush is a small town on the rugged West Coast of Ireland often lashed by the strong winds coming directly off the Atlantic Ocean.

The dream had started with me sat with my knees drawn up towards my chin, gazing down upon the town and its surroundings from the top of the hill that is just outside Kilrush on the Ennis Road. For a change, the breeze was soft, carrying with it the mixed odours of slightly acrid burning turf and the sweetness of horse manure. I was gazing down at the town over which the spire of St. Senan's Church pointed to sky, ready to take our prayers directly to heaven. Like a huge scar on the face of mother earth, Frances Street, the second widest street in all of Ireland, seemed to divide one third of the town from the rest. I wondered as to why this road had been built to such width considering its main traffic then was a few carts drawn by donkeys or horses.

To the far right from where I sat, with only fields beyond, almost as if the rest of the town was ashamed of its residents, ran Pound Street. Crossing Pound Street at The Cross was Pella Road. Officially, Pound Street was actually O'Gorman Street, but because it had once been the location of the town animal pound, virtually everybody referred to it as Pound Street. My life had revolved around 3 Pound Street and the Deloughery family that had lived there. I could see once more the Square, where Moore, John and Henry Streets met like tributaries of the river that was Frances Street.

At the bottom of Frances Street stood the reason for my being raised in Kilrush, Glynn's Flourmill. Just before it I could see the Monastery, once home of the most evil man I had ever met, Brother Walsh of the Christian Brothers. Perhaps he was at the root of my problem, but I didn't think so.

Raising my gaze, I see the modest harbour of Kilrush, demeaningly named by the locals The Creek. From this mere "creek" in the past, thousands of Irish families had boarded sailing ships that bore them across the Atlantic Ocean to the Promised Land called America. This was also the place where hundreds of Irish men and women were put aboard the prison ships in the 1830s and 40s under Trevalyan's Law. Trevalyan's Law stated that if you stole anything worth more than sixpence, there was no trial held and automatic deportation to Australia was your sentence. These prison ships left from the Customs House in the creek.

Skirting the creek, I see the narrow gauge railway line that carried us to Ennis, albeit slowly.

Raising my eyes further I can see the headlands of the Shannon Estuary where, on a clear day, there was no grander sight than watching the sun sink into the ocean beyond. I see the estuary of the River Shannon with its traffic of ships entering or leaving the mighty river that gave sea access to Limerick. In the estuary lay the low-lying islands of Scattery and Hog. On such a clear day I see the Kerry mountains, the beaches of North Kerry, and in the far distance the Ring of Kerry. Turning to my left I see a thick forest. Forest that went on for miles, providing a seemingly endless supply of timber to Doherty's sawmill that was located alongside The Creek. All of this was Kilrush, not then a town for tourists, rather one of scratching a living on a day-to-day basis.

I smiled as I recalled my dream, because it had contained a montage of characters that had formed my youth. My Auntie May, Uncle Andrew, their grown-up children, Joe Hawes, Johnny Enright, John Joe O'Shea and many others but most of all Paddy Griffin and his stories, jokes and memories that raised a smile from every one who knew and heard him.

I ceased remembering my dream and came back to the present. I took a sip of my whiskey. I could see the sky starting to lighten in the east, but I was not yet ready to return to my bed and sleep. As with most of us, I believed my childhood in Kilrush had been one of extreme happiness. But was it?

I had read somewhere that the child psychologist Watson said, "Give me the boy until seven and I will give you the man". According to his theory, a person's basic character is formed between birth and seven years of age. After that, you can educate but never alter the character of the person. If this were true, and as I had lived there until I was fifteen years of age, then my character had been formed in Kilrush. Perhaps something I was mentally suppressing had happened during that time that caused my occasional illogical unhappiness, perhaps not.

A friend of mine had once told me that if one had a problem, to write it down and then go to sleep. During your sleep, the mighty sub-conscience will pull together everything you have ever learned concerning that situation, and pass the result to your conscious. Sometime the following day, without knowing why, you would automatically know the best thing to do about that problem. Perhaps this would be the solution to my problem. I would have to face the ghosts of Kilrush and write down all I could remember.

As I finished my drink, I smiled. I distinctly felt I had heard the voice of my Uncle Andrew. "You've got to have a plan, Joe," he used to say. It was now light. I arose from the chair and decided there was to be no more bed for me, rather an early coffee. As I opened the sliding door to re-enter the house, I said out loud, "I've got a plan, Uncle Andrew. I am going to write down all I remember about my life in Kilrush. I will raise the ghosts of Kilrush and give them immortality and somewhere, as I face my childhood, walk through the lanes and the countryside of my town, sail and fish the rivers again, re-visit old friends from the past, I may just find myself along the way."

CHAPTER TWO

Gratefully Abandoned

I know when I came to Kilrush. I know how I came to Kilrush, but I had never been able to discover why I had been abandoned in Kilrush.

According to my birth certificate, I was born on the 9 August 1942, at 27, Skinner Street, in a small town called Thornaby-on-Tees. This is a town located in the northeast of England and situated in the smoke and smog of the industrial heartland of the Cleveland Valley, between Stockton and Middlesbrough, on the river Tees. People from this area are called 'Geordies', easily recognizable by their harsh dialect.

I remember very little of my early childhood in Thornaby-on-Tees, but I can remember the bombs and the noise they made. Thornaby was considered a prime target for the German Luftwaffe as it was the crossroads to the port of Tees Side and the giant steelworks of the Tees Valley. The Tees Valley was the heart of production for the army, navy and air force of Britain, and the aerodrome at Thornaby-on-Tees was home to the Spitfires, so we were prime targets most nights.

We lived about half a mile from the railway lines and the same distance from the aerodrome. There being no such thing as 'smart bombs' in those days, we tended to suffer what the Americans today describe as 'collateral damage.'

Some mornings, we would come home from the bomb shelters and find that all the windows in the house had been blown out by near misses. However, I do remember I had an older sister named May and a younger brother named David.

I remember it simply because I got into trouble when I washed David's hands and then dried them by putting them in the old-fashioned wringer. Well, it dried the sheets, didn't it? So why not hands? Anyway, David was stupid enough to cooperate.

The one occasion that I do remember was the victory party. The tables were put down the centre of the street. Flags and bunting were flying everywhere. We kids were given a feast and the whole neighbourhood danced and sang in celebration.

That street party stuck in my mind all these years. I remember my mother dancing with another lady in the street to the loud music. Everybody was so happy.

That was about all I could remember of my childhood years in Thornaby. I never went back to that street until many years later. I was about 15 when I went there just to re-visit where I was born. My family had then long since moved to 31, Beechwood Rd, which was about a mile away.

My father had been a sergeant in the Royal Engineers and had been stationed overseas for most of his service career, mainly in Egypt.

Late in 1945 my father was discharged from the British Army. In civilian life, my father was a flourmill engineer. The flourmill where he had worked was not far from home. In fact he could walk to the flourmill in about in 10 minutes. On his return to civilian life, he applied for a position with a different company in Manchester as a flourmill engineer, a position that would take him overseas. This was the beginning of his travels and his first assignment was to Kilrush to supervise the installation of machinery in Glynn's Flour-mill.

Early in 1946 my father returned on holiday from Kil-rush. I was about 3½ years of age at the time. He decided to take me with him when he returned to the site. For many years, I could not imagine as to why my mother agreed to such a thing. I was just an infant, at an age when a mother is needed; yet there my father was whisking me off to a strange country.

I was singled out and separated from my family. It certainly was a strange action to allow a child of such a young age to be taken away from his family and everyone he knew.

My early memories of Kilrush are not pleasant. My father had lodgings that consisted of one bed in the front parlour of a terraced house; the home of a lady called Mary Shalloe, at 2, Pella Rd. Mary was a widow and had a large family of her own. The house was a two-bedroom terrace house and very small considering the size of her family.

Every morning my father would leave for work at the flourmill, leaving me to my own devices. Every evening my father would come home from work, get washed and changed, then go to the local bar owned by his great friend, Frank McAuliffe and return at about midnight. In those days, "the bar was always open" and there were no times when the bar was closed, except of course for the Holy Hour. The Holy Hour was from 2:30 p.m. to 3:30 p.m. every day and it was stated that during this time of day you could not get a drink. Many people used to get a few drinks at 2:30 p.m. and make sure they lasted until 3:30 p.m. when the bar reopened.

My father always drank and showed a great capacity for taking alcohol. In fact, it was astonishing the amount of alcohol he could drink. He could drink beer and spirits as though there were no tomorrow.

Perhaps due to the stress of being away from my mother

and family, I was a bed wetter. This disturbed my father greatly, especially as he had to share the same bed with me. As soon as he came in and discovered I had wet the bed again, he would drag me from the bed and beat the living Jesus out of me. It seemed I did it every night, and so took beating after beating.

One night, when I was about four-years-old, he returned from the bar with a friend. I was fast asleep but had wet the bed. Perhaps because there was a witness to my demeanour was the reason he became even angrier than usual. Not only did he yank me from the bed and apply a terrible beating, but then he stripped off my clothes and threw me out of the house. I was out in the pitch black of night, cold, hurt and frightened. Even though somebody must have heard my cries, they were all too frightened of my father's fierce temper to give me assistance and take me in. The painful memories of those times have never left me.

The strange thing was many people in Kilrush had fond memories of my father. They remember him as a hugely friendly man, a great man to have a drink with, a man who never swore or blasphemed, and a great entertainer at the piano. Yet, this angel in the community became a child-beating devil once the door to his room was closed. Try as I might, I can never forgive him for the pain and anguish he inflicted upon me.

For such a young boy, it was not a happy time. It was a very lonely time. Although I lived in a house full of other children, I had no friends there. Children can be very cruel to each other if one is different from them, and I spoke with a Geordie accent, which to them was horrible. Not one of them wanted anything to do with me, so during the day I would wander the streets around the house, occasionally getting up to mischief.

Came 9 August in 1946, my fourth birthday. My father woke me and said he had bought me a donkey for my birthday.

I got dressed so fast, for I could see the donkey through the window and I was outside in a flash. I got a piece of rope and tied it around the donkey's neck. I then went for a walk out of the gate and up the road. Mary Shalloe had to go to the town that morning and get some shopping. When she came back I was in the kitchen sitting at the table with my donkey, having my breakfast. I was eating my cornflakes and the donkey beside me was enjoying the carrots I had put on a plate. Mary came through the door and I can picture her now. Mary was a middle-aged, grey-haired woman of more than ample proportions. When she saw the donkey, Mary let out a cry, "Jesus, Mary and Joseph" and started to laugh. She went out and got the neighbours to come and have a look at what was happening in the kitchen. May O'Donnell from the shop across the road, Sue from next door and Mrs. Maloney all come to have a look. Well the donkey had to have his breakfast and as far as I was concerned, having a donkey in the kitchen appeared to be the right and normal thing to do. I believe that Mary disagreed with having a donkey in the kitchen. It became one of the famous tales they used to tell about little Joe Riley, and when you look back I suppose it was funny.

It was about mid-morning that Mr. Kelly came looking for his donkey. It had gone missing and it now appeared that this was my "birthday present" from my father. Now arose a problem, Kelly wanted his ass back and I would not let it go. I know that I became very upset and was crying. They had to go to work and they could not work without the donkey. So a compromise was reached. I went with the Kelly's to work with the ass and spent the day riding on the donkey and cart. So all in all I had happy birthday in spite of being a butt of my father's idea of a joke. I ended up happily riding around the whole day with Kelly and his ass.

Without me knowing it, life was about to change dramatically for the better. It really started with a day trip.

Every Sunday, Frank McAuliffe would drive my father and me to Cappagh, where they would visit a bar and enjoy a few drinks. On this particular Sunday, there was another man in the car. He was a young man who worked with my father at the flourmill and his name was Sean Deloughery. Sean told me that he lived just behind us at 3, Pound Street. Throughout the journey both ways, Sean chatted pleasantly to me, and offered to make me a kite.

I was so excited about the thought of owning a kite that the next day found me sitting on a stone opposite the house of Sean hoping to see him. I had forgotten that he would be at work.

Every so often, a lady would come to the open door and stare out across at me. After a while, someone came out of the door and crossed the road and invited me into the house. Here, a kindly woman sat me down, gave me a cup of milk and some biscuits then asked who I was. I told her my name was Joe Riley, and that Sean had promised to make me a kite. She smiled kindly at me, and a feeling of security came over me. It was almost as if a weight had been lifted from me.

Eventually, Sean came in, smiling. Slowly the place filled up with the rest of the family, and they were all so nice to me. It was not long before I was calling the lady, "Auntie May," and she was to become the angel in my life, may she rest in peace.

The following day, I returned to visit my Auntie May. What a wonderful woman she was. I was made very welcome at the Deloughery household and everyday when I got up the first place I would go too was the Deloughery house and my Auntie May.

Auntie May always sat on a chair in the corner by the fire range. I would arrive and sit on her knee and she would give me a hug and a kiss. She would stroke my hair and hold me tight, I always felt secure when I was at Auntie May's.

Many years later and I found out the truth as to why I

was welcomed into the Deloughery household. Auntie May was a very religious woman; she prayed every day and went to confession every Saturday and Mass every Sunday. She had to go to confession because she swore like a trooper when she was mad, but a more loving person you could never wish to meet. I eventually learned that Auntie May had had a son whose name was also Joe. About two years before I arrived in Ireland, Auntie May's son was murdered at St. Senan's Well. He had been beaten to death with a club.

The loss of Joseph was a very hard thing for her to bear. This incident happened on St. Patrick's Day, the 17th March 1944. The assailant was never brought to justice and the case remained unsolved. At the time Joseph was only 17 years of age. While every year the town celebrated St. Patrick's Day with parades, concerts and much drinking, the house of Auntie May had the curtains drawn and was totally quiet in remembrance of Joseph. In my pre-teens I would sing solo in the annual St. Patrick's Day concert held in Mars Cinema. In spite of their deep love of me, neither Auntie May or any other member of the family witnessed my triumph on these occasions. Such was the depth of the grief of the family regarding their loss, that a day of joy had been lost forever. It was the only day in the year where the normally ever-open door was firmly closed against visitors, an action that was respected by all.

Then one day, a poor mite of a boy named Joseph, was sat alone on a stone staring at her house. To Auntie May, a very simple and religious woman who believed passionately in God and his Holy Mother, I had been sent by God to replace Joe, the son she had lost. Many times over the ensuing years she would look at me with a lot of sadness in her eyes.

I was spending more and more time at Auntie May's and was not being beaten by my father anymore as I would stay with Auntie May all day and night. At first, around 9 p.m. one of her sons, Willie, would take me home to Mary Shalloe's. He would leave me at the front of the house and I would run out the backdoor down the garden, over the fence, across the field and in the back door of Auntie May's before Willie got home. I would hide under the chair and behind Auntie May before Willie could catch me to take me back again. Auntie May would protect me. She would say, "Leave the poor cratter alone, will you?" I was then put to bed and I used to sleep with Sean.

I was unsure what my father was doing at this time. I don't think he really cared that I stayed with Auntie May. I presume that I was a bit of a burden to him and in a way I suppose he was glad that I was somewhere else and he had a dry bed to sleep in. I saw very little of him from then on. He was far too busy to visit me. Occasionally, someone would come to collect me to take me back to his digs, but Auntie May would always say that I was sick and they would leave me alone.

At Christmas time my father arrived to take me back to England. Auntie May was not happy at the thought of losing Joe again. Before my father arrived I was put to bed by Auntie May where she told me to be very sick and I played the part very well. My father did not take me back to England and neither did he return for many years.

I had found a whole family who loved me. Kilrush was to be my home for many years to come. My bedwetting ceased altogether.

The Deloughery family became a part of me over the next 12 years. They became my parents, my brothers, my sisters and those years were to be the happiest years of my life because I had known no other.

CHAPTER THREE

My New Home

The houses along Pound Street and Pella Road were mostly small terraced houses. Each house was painted in a different colour. Some houses were bright red, others blue, some green; in fact they were all the colours of the rainbow. You certainly didn't get bored walking down these streets. There also seemed to be dogs everywhere as well as donkeys and carts. With the cows, chickens, geese and the odd turkey floating around as well, the place was like a menagerie.

In most homes, ornaments and decorations were sparse, to say the least. When I first arrived in Kilrush all lighting was from oil lamps. Oil lamps still dominated until the late fifties as a lot of people could not afford electricity.

Every house in Kilrush had a picture of the Sacred Heart. This picture took pride and place in every home and had an oil lamp continually burning beneath it. Later on, when we eventually installed electricity, little electric lamps in the shape of a heart took over from the oil lamp and were left running 24-hours a day.

Other pictures on the wall were usually of distant family members, people who had died many years before. The photographs had mainly discoloured with age.

As in most other houses, our house had a statue of St. Jude, and he was the great saint for getting husbands, an essential to any household that had growing daughters.

Sean once commented, not within the hearing of Auntie May I hastily add, that he thought that St. Jude was a load of superstitious nonsense. Unfortunately, he made the remark to Paddy Griffin, who immediately started on one of his tales:

"Will you get away our dat. The power of St. Jude is well proven. Why, der is dis woman livin' not too far from here, but I won't mention her name as den you'd all know who I'm talkin' about.

"Well, wasn't she getting desperate to get married and start a family? And didn't she know just the man who would make her a happy woman?

"Every day, she would kneel in her parlour prayin' her heart out to St. Jude, beggin' him to deliver her man to her doorstep.

"Would you believe dat one day when she was prayin' didn't a wedding party pass her parlour window? And when she glanced out, who should be the groom but the very man she'd been beggin' of St. Jude to deliver to her. Well now, dis woman had a terrible temper she did. A grand rage she had worked before she had even got off her knees. She stood up, seized the statue of poor St. Jude and hurled him through the window with all of her might.

"It was a grand throw alright, but didn't yer man who was innocently passing by get struck on the head wid it? Down he went to his knees, clutching his poor old head.

"As the woman saw the poor man on his knees wasn't she filled with remorse for what she had done? She rushed out and helped him into her house, where she bathed his poor aching head. There they both were in the kitchen. She made him a cup o' tay and they chattered away for an hour or two.

Now they are married with three kids, so you see, St. Jude works alright, but sometimes in ways dat seem peculiar to you and me."

The area in which we lived was one of the poorest sections of town. In the Deloughery household though, we were reasonably well off. Well, there were many people who were less fortunate, at least. Most of the houses had an open fireplace as that not only provided heat but was the only means of cooking food, including bread. The fuel that was used was of course turf and we would have to get our own turf from the bogs. However, I don't think that anybody at our end of town went hungry. Everybody had a garden or a plot of land and in the spring and summer they would plant vegetables.

Most people, similar to us, had their own chickens to provide eggs and of course, everybody in the town used to fish, except for those who lived in the centre of the town in Frances Street, Henry Street or Moore Street. These people didn't need to fish as they were so well off they could afford to buy from others. So, I can say that the people at my end of town were never hungry, but then they also had few luxuries. The only luxury was a radio. We used to gather at O'Brien's house to listen to Michael Miles and his quiz program, Double Your Money.

During the 1940s and 50s life was hard in our end of town. Unemployment seemed to affect every house and a lot of young people had migrated to other countries to earn a living.

When you consider the harshness of the way people lived in those days, very little money, scraping an existence out of the land or the sea, yet nobody needed to be treated by a psychiatrist or file a suit for divorce. There has got to be a lesson somewhere in all of this. Society of those days, with all its harshness, had no divorce and if there was a psychiatrist in Kilrush, he would have starved to death from lack of patients.

Virtually all of the houses had roofs of thatch. We, on the other hand, had a modern kitchen range and a slate roof.

We also had our own horse and cart. The horse was a grey Connemara pony. I learned to ride on this pony and I always rode bareback simply because we could not afford a saddle. I still have a photograph of me stood on that horse's back at the age of five. Even at this age I handled a horse like a veteran. Every day it would be my job to ride the horse back to its paddock. Paddy Custy would ride on his bike behind me so after I had put the horse into the field, Paddy would bring me home on the crossbar.

At first, I didn't have any friends of my own age, but it didn't bother me. The few kids I tried to befriend always asked why I spoke so funny. It wasn't long, however, before my harsh Geordie way of speech was slowly replaced with the lovely west Clare lilt. Anyway, I could wander and explore my new territory at will. A child was safer in Kilrush than anywhere else in the world. There were so few motor vehicles on the roads that there was little chance of being run over. It was amazing in those early days at just how many adults would stop me on the street to ask who I was and where I lived. It seemed that in no time, everybody knew just who was little Joe Riley. It worked both ways, though. It didn't take Joe Riley long to know a lot of people, either.

Chapter Four

My Adopted Parents

For all of my adult life I believed God smiled upon me when that kindly lady I called Auntie May first opened her arms, hugged me to her bosom with the words, "You poor cratter." Auntie May took me into her home, but more importantly, into her heart. It was not because she was lonely, far from it. She had four sons and three daughters of her own, all but one living at home in that small cottage. She also had her husband, Uncle Andrew, as well as her brother Birdie, so named as he whistled all of the time. One would have thought that Auntie May would have wanted one less to look after, not one more.

Sleeping arrangements were cramped, to say the least. This was only a two-bedroom house. Our bedroom had two double beds and one single. Sean and I shared one bed, Willie and Gerard the other and Birdie on his own in the single bed.

In the front bedroom there were one single and a double bed. Mary and Katie slept heads and tails in the single bed. Uncle Andrew and Auntie May slept in the double bed but with Lulu at the bottom.

When I first arrived on the scene, Auntie May was a small, dumpy woman in her mid fifties. She always wore dark clothes protected by a wrap-around pinafore. She had very sharp features and her grey hair was always tied up in a bob, yet when she did let it down it would reach halfway down her back. Auntie May hardly ever appeared to rest. She was always busy cooking, cleaning or washing. Life in those pre-appliance days was very hard for a woman.

Although everybody in the house were devout Roman Catholics, Auntie May was more fervent than most. Not a Saturday went by when she did not go to confession. Not as though Auntie May had committed many sins, except that when aroused she could swear like a trooper. For all the Catholics in Kilrush, the confessional was the holy fire-escape. In our area, avoiding going to hell was more important than having money. Auntie May was determined that she would not go to hell. Paddy Griffin used to kid her a bit on this by saying to her, "When you die, may you be in heaven before the devil finds out."

On Sunday, of course, she would attend Mass, usually accompanied by most of the family. I was excused as I was probably the only Protestant in town, something that was to cause me a great deal of trouble in the years ahead.

Auntie May was a great cook and taught all the girls and one of her sons, Willie, the art of cooking.

Every morning she was up at the crack of dawn and she would start to make the bread. Bread was made fresh every day in this household and came in many forms. All the bread was soda bread made with buttermilk from the creamery. We had brown stone bread, white bread, and griddlecake. Homemade bread was the order of the day and as I got older I used to go to the creamery clutching three-pence in my hand to buy a bucket of buttermilk.

The griddlecake was usually made in the afternoon and was served hot. In the late forties you could only buy one type of bread from Maude Griffin's shop and that was a duck loaf. Auntie May would never buy it, however, preferring to make her own bread, fresh each and every day.

Auntie May was the leader of the household without a doubt. My Uncle Andrew, her husband, thought he ran the house but we all knew different.

Uncle Andrew, a quiet and very gentle soul, was born around the 1870s. As a young man he was a ship's carpenter in the Royal Navy. There was a photograph of him on the wall in Navy uniform. Uncle Andrew had joined the Royal Navy in 1911, together with his good friends from Kilrush, Paddy Griffin and Paddy Brasil. Surprisingly, they had generally managed to get berths on the same ships. They remained great shipmates all of their lives.

How Uncle Andrew survived being holed up in a ship for weeks on end with Paddy Griffin, I'll never know, although you couldn't help liking him. Paddy lived in the same street as us, opposite his sister Maude's shop; with his brother in a terraced house the same as ours.

Paddy was known as the local storyteller. He could spin a yarn and he could make you believe it. In fact, I think he had been telling the stories for so long that he believed them himself.

More commonly known behind his back as "Pollock the Liar" everybody knew and liked Paddy.

Paddy was very thin and stood about 5 feet 6 inches tall. He always wore a very old black suit with a waistcoat, a flat cap and a shirt with no collar. He was a carefree soul who had time for a yak and a yarn at any street corner and he possessed a great sense of humour.

His brother was a totally opposite character to Paddy, being quiet and hardly ever speaking a word. I suppose Paddy did enough talking for both of them. His opening statement was always, "Will you go away our dat" to most any conversation that was brought up. Whatever you had to say Paddy topped it with a better story.

When Paddy had drank a few pints of porter he would come to our home, up the path with his cap in hand and tap on the door for a chat with Uncle Andrew. "God bless all here," he would say as the door was opened. He would then sit down behind the door and get out his packet of Woodbines, always a packet of five, and then complain about the price of three-pence that he had paid his sister Maude, who owned the shop opposite his house.

Uncle Andrew, a non-drinker, was not always happy about Paddy's visits, as Paddy had usually had a few jars and he had heard the stories a hundred times before.

"Paddy, will you have a cup o' tay?" Auntie May would ask.

"No thank you ma'am." Paddy would reply. "Are you trying to ruin my reputation?"

Uncle Andrew and Paddy would talk a while, usually the gossip that spreads through any small town, but eventually the talk would turn to reminiscing about their days serving together in the Royal Navy.

This would set Paddy off telling us some of the stories. One I remember well was where the three of them were selected to be in the team that was to pull the coffin of King George V in the State funeral.

"You should have seen it," said Paddy . "It was a grand show. There we three were, all stood to attention outside Buckingham Palace waiting to be called to pull the carriage. Alongside me was the new king's younger brother, the prince, in his full dress uniform. On the steps was King Edward with his mother, the widowed Queen. It was a grand sight," continued Paddy, with all of us sat on the floor at his feet, entranced.

"Suddenly," said Paddy. "The Queen lifts her hand and points in our direction. "Who is that there?" she asks King Edward. "Why," he answered. "That's Paddy Griffin." The Queen turned and gave him a weird look. "I know that is Paddy Griffin," she said. "But who is the person next to him with the flat cap and all the medals?"

Uncle Andrew, Paddy Brasil and Paddy Griffin had all been involved in the Battle of Jutland. It must have been a frightening experience, as nobody ever heard them talk about it. The closest to any mention of the North Sea was when Paddy told another of his stories.

"Well, here we were on a little destroyer, being chucked around like a cork," started Paddy. "I was on watch and didn't I spot me a German submarine. I shouted and we turned towards it, but it went under the water."

"Backward and forward we went, searching all the time for dat submarine, but nothing. It was awful frustrating. I went to the captain and told him the only way we were going to find it was if I went overboard and searched. Three full days I am swimming around and then, would you believe it? The submarine surfaced right next to me. I waited. The hatch cover opened and two officers came out. Wasn't it just my luck that the captain spotted me?" Paddy would then take a big breath to let it sink in. We all wanted to hear the finish. "The captain looked me straight in the eye and shouted, 'Jesus Christ. It's Paddy Griffin. Doive, doive, doive,' and wouldn't you know, we lost him."

When I was six years of age, Uncle Andrew introduced me to fishing. When he finished making my fishing rod, he put me on the crossbar of his bike and we cycled all the way out to Cappagh. It was one of those nice spring afternoons with the blue sky and a light breeze coming in from the Shannon. We set up the fishing rod with hook and float.

After Uncle Andrew had given me a few lessons, I cast my line out into the water and watched with excitement and anticipation. It was not long before we got a bite and sure enough the float disappeared under the water, I had strain on the line and I could feel the fish pulling away and dragging the line from side to side. Eventually Uncle Andrew had to intervene. I was not even strong enough to take this fish out of the water. I could see the flashing white of the fish as it criss-crossed under the water. Uncle Andrew slowly but surely started to pull the fish in. He got it near the wall of the pier and said, "Joe. You have a lovely fish here. It's a whiting." The fish weighted in at about four pounds, not bad for my first time fishing.

Uncle Andrew treated me like the grandson he never had. He loved me and I loved him so much. I was his pride and joy and he took me everywhere with him. He also had a broken heart for the Joseph he lost but loved the Joseph he found.

Uncle Andrew must have been a very fit man because I can remember one day I sat on the crossbar of his bike and he cycled the ten or so miles to Kilkee. At this stage he must have been in his late sixties or early seventies and most people of today would not even contemplate cycling from Kilrush to Kilkee. That was a gruelling exercise cycling up and down those hills especially with me on the crossbar.

Uncle Andrew had some relatives in Kilkee, the Haugh family. I didn't know a great deal about them because I was too young, however Paddy Haugh was a barber and he used a cut Uncle Andrew's hair. After his haircut we would get on the bike and cycle all the way back to Kilrush.

CHAPTER FIVE

Infant School

In the parish of Kilrush there were four schools; a school in the convent, where the girls suffered their own injustices under the strict regime of the nuns; the National School and the Christian Brothers School. Both of the latter were staffed and run by the Christian Brothers. The fourth school was on the Scattery Island. The children of Scattery were very fortunate as none of their teachers were Christian Brothers or nuns.

Throughout my school days, not just in the infants, I was to painfully discover that the term 'Christian Brothers' was an oxymoron. If one is to believe the Holy Bible, Christians do not deliberately inflict pain and torture on other human beings, let only young children.

Having spent a great many years within their sphere of influence, I now believe that the main qualification for being a Christian Brother was firstly to hate children and secondly to have basic training by either the Gestapo or the SS.

They believed that they had the responsibility of dispensing God's justice and punishment to all children in their care. They systematically inflicted physical as well as mental torture on all.

My first-year teacher was Mrs. Finucane. Mrs. Finucane was a beautiful lady with blue eyes, blonde hair, and a very gentle nature. She cared for us and in her own way appeared to love all of her charges. Maybe she was aware of what was about to befall us when we went to the next stage of education and therefore took pity on us. The year that we spent with this teacher led us into a false sense of security, for beyond that year laid an education system that would test and frighten anyone on this planet.

When I left Mrs. Finucane's class, I was again lulled into a false sense of security as our teacher was Brother Conway.

He was a giant of a man, but like most large men, he was a gentle person. Perhaps because of this, after a few short weeks he was posted far away to another school. I was to see him only once after this, and that was at the consecration of St. Senan's Well. For his replacement the education system inflicted upon us a Christian Brother who was undoubtedly the most vicious individual that a six-year old child could encounter.

His name was Brother Walsh. Brother Walsh was a small man about 5 feet 6 inches tall, with a wizen face sporting broad black glasses. He was slim and always clean-shaven. Brother Walsh always wore the long black flowing gown of the Brotherhood, together with a white half collar around his neck. Hanging from his belt would be a long set of black Rosary beads, while tucked in the belt would be his favourite weapon, a black leather strap. This strap was one of the weapons that he used to dispense God's justice and punishment.

Brother Walsh is burned into my memory and will never be forgotten. His brutality, his cruelty and his maltreatment's in the name of his God were unmerciful.

Brother Walsh could never be accused of having favourites because he brutalized every child in the class.

Brother Walsh singled me out for special treatment. He made my life so hard and miserable over the next year.

According to Brother Walsh, I had two major flaws and

he insured that the rest of the class and the school were made aware of them.

First, I had been born in England, a country hated by many Irish people because of the British occupation for 800 years and the then fairly recent persecution by Winston Churchill (called John Bull) using the Black and Tans. The latter incidents were very fresh in the minds of the people of the town. Secondly, I was a Protestant in an all-Catholic school. In fact, I may have been the only Protestant in the town, and this caused me much grief.

Brother Walsh made sure that other members of my class knew I was not the same as they by refusing to allow me to be part of religious studies. Every school day from 11:30 a.m. until 12:30 p.m. there was a period for religious education. He would call me out each and every day and say "Riley. You can go home." You do not have to be a genius to understand what happened. I became a small boy who was picked on and ridiculed by everyone in school.

I now became a fighter because it was the only way to survive. My attitude was; "Yes, you can pick on me, call me a proddie, call me John Bull, or whatever. However, I don't care who you are or how big you are, I will take you on." I had to take on all comers because if I did not I was done for in this small community.

I was not a tall boy but I was well built and could run like the wind. I was athletic in that I played all games at school and always played to win. I never accepted second place and I have never given up at any time in my life since, so a hard lesson was learned in these early years.

Brother Walsh ensured that I had lots of practice at fighting both in and out of school. This is how I got my name and why I was singled out as a troublemaker when really, beneath it all, I just wanted to be left alone to live a normal life and survive. At the end of the day the other boys just gave up because I was not going to lie down for anyone.

They soon learned that one way or another I was going to inflict some measure of pain on them, even if I lost.

One boy I met was due to one of these encounters, defending myself, and he became my good friend for many years. His name was Paddy Enright.

Paddy was about two years older than me and a big lad for his age. Paddy lived down our lane with his family and one day I was playing near his house. I think I was throwing stones at the windows of the old flourmill that was derelict. Paddy was sent out by his older brother to chastise this young English hooligan. Paddy was unaware of my reputation. He proceeded to beat me and I ended up with a black eye and a bleeding lip. I took quite a bit of punishment from Paddy before I hit him over the head with a plank of wood. This stopped Paddy in his tracks, he was bleeding from a wound in his head and it shook him. Paddy never picked on me again. There was no other way of survival for a young Protestant boy in a very prejudiced society.

I do not think it is hard to understand that I did not have a great respect for God's representatives on earth considering the terrible things that they inflicted on me during my school days.

On occasions, someone in the classroom would speak and Brother Walsh would take his leather strap and throw it at the individual. He would then request the individual to bring it back to him and he would announce that should any other child speak, then the whole class would be punished. Brother Walsh was always true to his word. He enjoyed mass punishment of young children because he was a sadistic bastard. When the next person in the class spoke, he would get all of us out in a line and proceed to administer God's justice, as interpreted by Brother Walsh.

The mass punishment was carried out in the following fashion. He would put a stool against the wall. Everybody had to jump over the stool, and whilst they jumped and their knees were bent, he would lash their buttocks with a cane. Once he had completed punishment for everybody, he would turn us all around and inflect the same punishment once more. Brother Walsh was an expert at handing out mass punishment to small boys.

Brother Walsh's expertise of applying not just physical, but mental violence to young children had no equal among men. One particular incident clearly showed that not only was he not Christian, but that he was also a disgrace to the human race.

This incident involved a little six-year-old boy called Michael Casey. Michael came from the other side of the town, living on Grace Street that was down near the woods. Grace Street was one of the country's first efforts to house Travelling people, who for many generations had wandered the roads of Ireland doing odd jobs. Perhaps his background was the reason Brother Walsh hated him above others. Michael Casey will live in my memory always because of the injustice that happened to him, and because of what a so-called Christian person did to him.

Michael almost invariably was late for school. Maybe, like most of us, he had chores to be completed before he left for school, but for whatever reason, he rarely arrived before 9:30 a.m. in the morning.

One cold winter morning, Michael arrived late as usual. In spite of the temperature, Michael was only wearing shorts, a shirt over which was an old jumper that sported so many holes it could not have provided much warmth. He was also bare-footed.

Michael stood there just inside the door of the classroom.

Brother Walsh looked at him through his glasses with a glare that we all knew so well. When we saw him in that mood he was frightening and we knew something was about to happen.

"Michael Casey," he intoned. "You will never be late for school again." He went behind the blackboard and emerged holding an air rifle. He repeated to Casey, "You will never be late for school again," and he pointed the rifle at his head. Brother Walsh walked towards him with the rifle pointed at him and Casey backed up. You could see the fear in his eyes as he backed between the desks. The silence and fear in the classroom was horrific.

Brother Walsh put his foot on the chair and then stepped up unto the top of the desk. He walked across the top of the desks, all the time pointing the gun at young Casey's head and shouting at him. Casey eventually could go no further, he was backed up against the wall and Brother Walsh towered over him with the gun still pointed at his head.

During this entire facade, one must remember that we were children just six years of age. Brother Walsh was a monster of a man in any society and as far as we were concerned Casey was about to be murdered. Brother Walsh again reiterated, "Casey you will never be late for school again" and at this point he pulled the trigger—and there was the loudest click that I have ever heard in my life.

Sad to say, Michael Casey never attended school again. I used to see him down in the woods on occasions, but he never came back to school. What a terrifying experience for a 6-year-old boy and his classmates. What sort of an animal was this inhumane bastard of a man and who let him loose on a group of young children?

It would appear that to Christianity, religion and God, Michael Casey meant very little. I don't think that this so-called Christian Brother cared one little bit for anyone or anything. Michael Casey came from the wrong side of town and the fact that he could not read, write or do anything else was of no consequence to this individual teacher.

I remember going home at lunchtime, like all the children in the school, and telling the story of how Brother

Walsh threatened to shoot Casey. I presume that all the children told the same story at home as I did. However the Christian Brothers were held in such reverence by the town's people, not one person spoke up for young Michael Casey and the atrocity that had befallen him.

During the year, we had a stroke of good luck. Brother Walsh was transferred to India. We had no idea how long it took to get to India or to get back; however we were reliably informed that it would take at least three to four weeks for Brother Walsh to get there. On the day he left, we were all lined up outside the school to wave Brother Walsh farewell. I was at the forefront of the waving and shouting with joy, full knowing that we would not see this man for at least two months.

I have on many occasions thought about those poor children in India that would be subjected to this so called Christian, for surely they had less than we did and must have been subjected to the horrors of this individual who was there in the name of God.

Brother Walsh was my induction to an education system that for the next few years could only be described as brutal. A system that was so corrupt yet conducted its affairs in the name of religion and its God.

Brother Walsh was an evil man totally unsuited for the teaching or preaching profession. Unfortunately, as I was to discover in primary school later, he was to prove the rule rather than the exception in the Christian Brothers sect. Little did we know then, living in our small corner of Ireland, that the Christian Brothers were brutalizing children in their schools all over the world! I thank God that all over the world this was eventually exposed, publicized and stopped, with many victims being financially compensated. Unfortunately compensation cannot restore the loss of a normal childhood.

CHAPTER SIX

The Number One Son

Fortunately for me, every afternoon and at weekends, I could escape from the brutality of school and return to the sanity and love of my adopted family, the Delougherys. The eldest son of Auntie May was Gerard.

Gerard was in his early thirties, he was portly had the sharp facial features of the Delougherys family. He was about 5 feet 7 inches tall and worked in Glynn's flourmill. Gerard was no match for Paddy Griffin, but he had a quick sense of humour. Once, when Auntie May had asked me to go and buy "one stone of potatoes," as I was going out the door, Gerard said.

"Make sure you don't buy the big ones, Joe."

I stopped and turned to him. "Why not?" I asked.

"Because you'll find them too heavy to carry," he replied.

Gerard worked shifts and if he was on the afternoon shift, I would take his tea down to the flourmill after I arrived home from school.

As I entered the house, Auntie May would be sat in her favourite chair in the corner, enjoying her cup of tay. "Joe," she would say. "Will you take Gerard his tay?"

Auntie May would make the tea in an enamelled can with a lid on it. The lid could be used as a cup, but Gerard preferred to drink out of a mug, so I would carry one for him to use. I would walk to the mill, which was only five minutes away, and go through the office door, and then turn left to the big fire door. Being so small, I had to get someone to open this door for me because it was so heavy. Once past this door the noise was deafening. I would cross the floor and up the stairs. On the first floor was John Houlihan, who lived next door to us, while Gerard was on the floor above him.

Gerard would be tending his machines that made the flour and everything seemed to be covered in a fine dust of flour. You would get it on your clothes and hands.

I would sit on the steps and wait. Gerard would come with that big smile on his face.

"How are ya Riley," he'd say. "Here, sit up on the window."

He would lift me up onto the windowsill and I could look out across the creek and see what was happening. I could see Jack Hanrahan with his horse and cart at the town refuse tip that was located behind Ryan's warehouse on the dock.

Jack Hanrahan was sometimes called Jack the Turnip on account of his balding head that could only be seen if he took his cap off, which was not often. Jack was a council worker, but the most conscientious man you could every meet and in fact, the only person who worked for the council.

Jack was a kind man. If I was out at Cappagh or up the town I would often hop on the cart and he would give me a lift home. Jack was in his fifties, of slim build but a wiry character and full of life. As he would pass me by he would say, "Riley. How are ya?"

I would reply, "Grand, Jack. And how's yourself?" He would pass by with a touch of his hat.

Jack had a horse and cart and it was his job to clear the drains, the ditches, the roads and pick up the rubbish from the cans and bins left out.

He had a special day for picking up the rubbish down

Pound Street and Pella Road. However, Jack was always ready to rest on the cart or his shovel and talk with anybody passing by. Jack knew everything that was going on in the town and was an expert on human nature. Jack lived in Pella Road and was known by everybody in the town. On his days off Jack could be seen to be moving furniture. Jack was the only available house-mover in the town of Kilrush.

Jack also liked to have his jar of stout, in other words his pint of Guinness and on many occasions Jack could be seen going home, sitting in his cart fast asleep and the only one who knew where he was going was the horse. You would see Jack coming down past the handball alley, the reins hanging down. The horse would walk slowly past our house and it was as if the horse knew it had to go slow so as not wake Jack up. They would pass Maude Griffin's shop, wander passed Pa Scanlon's little cottage, turn right at The Cross then up Pella Road. The horse would stand outside his house and someone would eventually come out and take Jack in.

Sat in the window of the flourmill, I could sometimes watch the engine of the West Clare Railway shunting up and down the dock. I could see the boats tied up on the dock wall. There was Ryan's boat, the St. Senan, and Glynn's boats the Atlita and the Dingle. The dock was always a busy place with lots happening. From this window you could see Scattery Island and the Shannon estuary with some big ships on their way to Limerick.

I could look at the railway station below and follow the line out past the quay and the signal box at the bottom of the Shanakyle Road with the gates going down to the Customs House and the seaweed factory. I could also see the engine sheds behind Mrs. Black's house and the lines following the quay all the way out to Scough Point and beyond.

Auntie May always put a piece of bread in the bag for me. Gerard would have his tea in his mug and I would have some tea in the top of the tea can. Gerard and I would talk about where we would go the next week on the motorbike.

Gerard's hobby in the early years was greyhound racing and breeding. He had a few different greyhounds but somehow they never did much until he bought a pair from a farmer in Doonbeg. He registered them and called them Confident Liz and Confident Leash. Liz was the better of the two and she won the Kilkee Cup, and that was a big day, for at last Gerard had a winner. We used to walk for miles over the fields at the back of the house. The hounds would be on a single lead with a release trigger on it.

Accompanying us would be Rebel, a small black hunting dog. He would flush out the rabbits and hares. As soon as he got the rabbits on the run, Gerard would release the dogs and the hunt would be on. It was always good if we got a hare out in the open field as the dogs would have a good chance of getting him before he got to the bushes.

Gerard's other love in life was motorbikes. He sold the hounds and purchased a motorbike. His first motorbike was a 250 c.c. BSA and we went for miles on this bike. He later got a 350 c.c. and this was his dream bike. He bought it from a man in Wexford who advertised it in the newspaper. Gerard spoke with him on the telephone and bought the bike sight unseen. The motorbike was delivered by rail and we went down to the station and waited for the little West Clare railway train to come in with his precious load. The train arrived and the motorbike was in the baggage car. It was a big red machine that had suspension both front and rear. We rolled the motorbike down the station platform and out the gate to the road. Gerard got on the motorbike, switched on the petrol, gave it a kick and away she went. He rode a hundred yards to the bottom of Frances Street, in front of the mill. He then went up Frances Street and out onto the Cappagh Road. I could hear the roar of the motorbike as he went past Doherty's timber yard. He came back after a few minutes and I hopped on the back and we rode the motorbike home for everyone to see.

When Gerard was on the morning shift he would come to the school and pick me up. I would walk out the gate and sure enough there was Gerard waiting for me on his motorbike. We didn't have helmets as I don't think they had been marketed at the time. I usually wore my hat that came down around my ears to keep them warm. We would head off up to Kilkee and on to Doonbeg. At Doonbeg we would go to the Blue Hole and sometimes we would catch some fish. When the tide went out it would expose a number of very deep holes in the rocks and occasionally some very nice fish would be left stranded in them ready for the picking.

Some days we used to go to the Cliffs of Moher beyond Liscannor in North Clare. The Cliffs of Moher are one of the highest sea cliffs in Europe and were rarely visited in those days. We would lie down on our stomachs and crawl out to the edge to look down at the Atlantic Ocean below. We could clearly see the Aran Islands straight ahead and the Galway Mountains to the north.

In April and May we used to go and watch the basking shark. They used to follow the Gulf Stream and you could not count the vast number of sharks. We would watch them roll, and as they rolled you could see their teeth. It's a shame that today you go to the Cliffs of Moher but the basking shark are no more. They have been hunted to near extinction. The Cliffs of Moher, where once there was nothing but the wild barren land, has today been taken over with shops selling souvenirs and restaurants. The last time I went there in 1968, I could not believe what they had done to this most beautiful place. It appears that nothing is sacred anymore in this modern world and places of beauty like this have to be clogged by cars, buses and hundreds of people with cameras and bags. I could not go back there again and see what they have done. Many years ago it was wild and beautiful. One could look across the cliffs and there would not be a person to be seen. I suppose it holds some beauty today for those hoards of people who go to see it, but somehow it has lost its magic for me. I think if Sean and Gerard were alive today they would be very sad at what they saw at these cliffs and the way they have changed so much.

Gerard earned about one pound five shillings a week and this was for a six-days a week and eight hours a day on shift work in the mill. As he neither smoked nor drank, all he needed was enough for a tank of petrol and he was happy. He was a grand fellow, and always a pleasure to be with.

CHAPTER SEVEN

Sean, My Hero

S ean was my hero, he looked after me, cared for me and he was my "big brother." The only vice he had was smoking. He was the most gentle of people that you could ever meet in this life. He never raised his voice and I don't think I ever saw him angry with anyone or anything.

Sean, in his own way, was like a big kid. Every night he would go to the movies. He didn't like the big pictures as such, but he loved the cartoons. He loved them all, including Mickey Mouse, Donald Duck, and Bugs Bunny. His favourite though was Tweety Pie and Sylvester the Cat. Sean's laughter would fill the cinema. When he came home at night from the pictures and I was then only four or five years of age, he would bring a bar of chocolate and one of his favourite comic books. He would get into bed. I would wake up and we would share the chocolates and read the Beano or the Dandy. Our favourite character in the comic was Desperate Dan and, of course, Superman.

Sean loved fishing and he took over where Uncle Andrew left off. He would put me on the handlebars of the bike and we would cycle over to the woods and fish. We would fish for hours for the brown trout and we would make all our own flies. In those days the nearest fishing tackle shop was in the city of Limerick 70 miles away and we went there only once a year at Christmas. I remember some of the flies were so beautiful and colourful. Sean would sit at night-time and make these beautiful flies. Flies like the March Hare, which had colours of orange and blue.

Sean and I would walk along the banks of the river among the trees in the woods, so peaceful that all that you would hear was the wind rustling through the leaves. I really enjoyed fishing with Sean. We would take some milk in a bottle and some sandwiches to eat when we were hungry.

Whenever I got new toys, Sean would always play with them first. One year I was given a Meccano set for Christmas. It was a big one and was sent from England by my mother. Sean and I spent all-day making cars, making cranes and anything else that would work with wheels on. Another Christmas I received a Hornby electric train set and that was great. When Sean went to Limerick he would buy something to add onto the railway set.

One really good project was a joint venture between Sean and Uncle Andrew. They made me this beautiful red model sailing boat. Uncle Andrew lovingly carved the hull from a single piece of wood. Into his work went the experience of all his years spent as a ship's carpenter. As it neared completion, Uncle Andrew would take down the bathtub from where it hung on the outside of the scullery wall, fill it with water and study the flotation. After, he would take his tools and carefully trim it even more. This was a boat built for speed. It was slick and looked great.

He then used small pins gently hammered in around the freeboard. The cotton thread he used to loop between the pins provided a grand handrail. Uncle Andrew took great care in carving the mast.

Sean, the engineer in the family, made a self-steering system linked to the tiller. He milled it down at the engineering shop at the old mill. Katie made the sails on her sewing machine and the hull was painted red with a white stripe along the side. It was a work of love by both Uncle Andrew and Sean. Katie smiled all the time she was working on the sails.

When it was finished, we all gazed lovingly upon it. It was not just a toy yacht, but a real work of art.

Came the day for the first run and testing of this magnificent vessel. Off we went down to the quay. After a great debate between Uncle Andrew and Sean, it was decided to launch our boat from the slip that was halfway down the quay by Ryan's warehouse. The consensus was that it would stop somewhere within the harbour and we would just go and recover it.

The yacht was sailing great, travelling fast, keeled over in the wind and headed straight out to the boathouse. Uncle Andrew got on his bike. With me on the cross bar we cycled down the Cappagh Road to the boathouse. As we were going up the hill past the turn-off to Barrack Hill, we could see the yacht still going on its direct course, and travelling at a great rate of knots.

We got to the boathouse just in time—time that is to see it pass us by. It was now on a direct course to the Atlantic Ocean. We started to throw stones at it to get it to turn, but with no success.

We all stood silent on the pier of the boathouse and watched our beautiful yacht sail into the sunset between the heads. We never saw it again.

Being made of solid wood, my yacht would never have sunk. It had to land somewhere. So, if in the late 1940s you found a small red yacht on the east coast of the USA or on the sands of Ballybunion, would you please send it back to me?

Sean had a terrible sweet tooth. He couldn't resist chocolates, cakes or ice cream. He always had something in his pocket and I always helped him out by eating my share.

Sean by trade was not just an engineer but a good engineer. He had the ability to fix anything that was mechanical. He had learned his trade while serving in the Irish Army.

When he first came home he had worked in the flour-mills with my father. Later, he became a ship's engineer on the boats travelling to Limerick and back. During my summer holidays, I was allowed to make these trips with him. Sean loved the sea and so did I.

Sean and I travelled the Shannon River together on the Dingle, carrying flour from Kilrush to Limerick, a trip of about five to six hours. We shared a very small bunk. This little trader had a crew of three, Sean, the Engineer; Mick Brasil, the seaman and Paddy Galvin the Captain.

We always preferred to make our journey upriver on an incoming tide. Kilrush Creek was very shallow at low tide. At certain times, if we waited at the quay for sufficient water to be under us to make way, we would not get started until late morning. On the occasions when this was likely to occur, we would take the boat out of the Creek in the late afternoon and anchor her at the Cappagh. This ensured that we could get an early start the following morning.

Sean and I would get our bags full of food, (no food was supplied by owners of these little boats) and, because it cut the corner off at Doherty's Mill and was a shorter route, walk out along the railway line to Cappagh at four in the morning. It was already light in the summer months and we would see the morning star shining so brightly. When we got on board Sean would busy himself in the engine room and I would put away the food. I was the unpaid cabin boy and loved every single minute of it.

The incoming tide would race up the River Shannon, and on good days, if we caught it at the right time, we could get to Limerick in less than five hours.

Once under way, everybody would be on the bridge. Sean would, at regular intervals; drop below to check on his beloved engines, but there was rarely any problem.

I would ask him, "Sean. How are we goin' for time?"

I would love it when he replied, "She's ripping along at the moment, Joe. At this rate we can have a rest this afternoon, and then we will go to the pictures. You'd like that?"

Of course I liked it. Limerick had a huge picture house. "Can we go and look at some fishing rods, Sean?" I would ask.

"Sure." answered Sean. "We'll go to that shop next to Woolworth's on the main street.

"Joe," interrupted Captain Paddy. "How about a cup of tay?"

"Aye, aye sir," I would answer with pride, then shoot off down the ladder to what passed as the galley. The galley had a small turf pot-bellied stove. The chimney pipe passed up and through a skylight. The fire was rarely allowed to go out, so all I had to do was give it a good poking and add another turf sod. Didn't that turf fire give out a grand smell?

While I was waiting for the kettle to boil, I would cut and butter some bread, and add the slices of home-cooked ham or cheese that Auntie May had given us that morning. I would take this first to the bridge, and then make the tea. Good and strong, just as we all liked it. When it had steeped, I would pour it into the chipped, enamel mugs. For me, the best was to come, for while Captain Paddy and his crew enjoyed their refreshment, I would be allowed to take over and steer the ship.

Because we were a lot faster, sometimes we would pass the St. Senan on her way up the river and we would hail Dan Ryan, the skipper.

We would stay in Limerick for three days, unload first then load up with whatever had to be brought back to Kilrush. We nearly always travelled through the night going back to Kilrush in order that the workers on the dock could start to unload and load again first thing in the morning. This, of course depended on the tides being right, but most times we would arrive between eleven at night and four in the morning.

My summers were beautiful, travelling the Shannon River between Limerick and Kilrush. It was a great experience. In later years, Sean went on the larger ships that travelled to Europe and England.

I was so lucky to have as my mentor Sean and while he never said it, because it was not the manly thing to do, I know he loved me very much. He would toss my hair, smile and put his arm around me, especially when I was frightened in bed.

All of the Deloughery brothers took the pioneer pledge, an oath that is given in church where one swore never to drink alcohol. A pioneer pin was then worn that signified you were a non-drinker.

Paddy Griffin used to say, "Will you get away wid our dat. Sure and don't I feel sorry for dose dat have taken the pledge? Every day when dey wake, dat is goin' to be the best dey feel all day. Sure, and when I wake up, don't I know dat I'm bound to feel better as the day goes on?"

I think Sean, unlike the other boys, broke his pledge in the first year. Gerard, Willie and Andrew never drank but Sean would have a drink possibly every six months. I only ever saw him drunk once and that was at Katie's wedding. I never knew him to have a girlfriend and his only real friend, when I think of it now, was me. His family, his brothers and sisters were his life. He took very little interest in anyone outside of the family. Sean may have been short on stature, about five foot six inches, but his heart filled all of his body.

CHAPTER EIGHT

Learning From A Wise Man

Uncle Andrew and I went on many a fishing expedition. There were two types of fishing that we did; the sea fishing from the pier or a boat and the fresh water fishing when we went looking for brown trout in the local rivers and lakes.

Uncle Andrew taught me the art of fly-fishing and this became one of my favourite sports in later life. If you walk down Frances Street in Kilrush and turn left at the bottom, just before the creek, there is a little bridge just at the start of the Cappagh Road. If you look over the wall on your left-hand side, there is a small river that flows over the dam wall. There is a plaque on that bridge commemorating Martin Frank McMahon, who drowned while trying to save the life of Frank McAuliffe. Frank was the son of my father's best friend, also Frank McAuliffe. The accident was caused when Frank and his pal Gerry McDermott were both on a bicycle riding at speed down Frances Street. The bike had no brakes and ran straight into the creek. His pal was saved, which was probably the reason he later became a priest. Martin Frank having witnessed the accident, bravely dived into the water to try to help them, but was himself drowned in that brave act.

I learnt all of my fishing skills on this little river. I have walked for miles up that river and through the woods catching the brown trout. Most summer evenings, just before dusk when the trout began to bite, would find me in the field close to the dam casting my line into the river.

Uncle Andrew had lots of ways to catch the trout and he taught me most of them.

The best one was using a sheep's head. One day, Uncle Andrew sent me up to the butcher's for a sheep's head. As I set off, Gerard with his usual sense of humour, shouted after me, "Joe. Tell them to leave the eyes in will ya?"

"What for?" I'd shouted back.

"Because it's got to see us through the week," was the reply.

Uncle Andrew had given me no clue as to why we needed a sheep's head. By the time I returned with it, the blood had soaked through the brown paper wrapping. Uncle Andrew got out his bike, I sat on the cross bar and off we went to the woods. We went way up to the back of the woods to a very quiet place that was difficult to get to.

"What are we doing?" I asked Uncle Andrew.

"Well, Joe. We are going to catch some really good trout here," was the reply.

"How are we going to do that, Uncle Andrew?" I asked. "We haven't even brought our rods."

"Joe," he replied. "This is called planning. We will be back here in a week to do some fishing."

When we reached the riverbank, Uncle Andrew unwrapped the sheep's head, and then from his pocket he produced a coil of thin wire. He threaded the wire through the head, and then tied it off.

"Now, Joe," he said. "See that branch there, the one that goes out over the river?" I nodded. "I want you to climb out on that branch with the sheep's head. I'll tell you where to stop. Then I want you to lower the head until it is three feet above the water, and after that, make the wire firm to the branch. Do you understand?"

I climbed out onto the branch and did as I was told. The sheep's head was just right. I secured the wire and crawled back to Uncle Andrew.

Uncle Andrew looked pleased. "That's grand," he said.

"What happens now, Uncle Andrew?" I asked.

"Well, Joe," he answered. "That head will start to rot pretty fast and the maggots will form and fall into the water. The trout down the river will know there is a good feed up here and will come up to have a look, and then we will be here waiting for them in a weeks time."

He then turned, and pointing at a spot in the river about 20 yards away, said, "Joe. Can you see that pool in the bend down there?" I nodded. "Well. That will be full of fish in a week and we will come up here with the rods. You see Joe, in life you always have to plan ahead"

Uncle Andrew told me this so many times as a boy. He used to say, "Joe. Every one has a plan whether they like it or not. If you do nothing you have a plan to fail. Always plan ahead."

We sat down with our backs resting against a tree. It was a beautiful day with only a gentle breeze making the trees whisper their secrets to each other. The river ran peacefully on to the sea, and the gentle damp smell of the weed caressed our nostrils. Just above the lush green grass, insects dodged to and fro. Occasionally a bird would call with a tuneful chirrup, seeking another of its species. All in all, a grand day indeed.

Uncle Andrew continued his lesson in planning by referring to his days in the navy. "When we were on sailing ships, the Master of the ship had only four questions in his planning.

The first was where are we now?

The second was where do we want to be?

The third was how can we get there?

And the final was, what is the best way for us to get there?"

He paused to allow what he had just said sink into my brain. Such a setting as this was meant for the passing on of wisdom.

"Where are we now?" he continued. "Well we might be in Liverpool. And where do we want to be? Let's say Australia. How can we get there? Well there are lots of different ways of getting to Australia. One is to round the Cape of Good Hope in South Africa. Or maybe round Cape Horn, that's a bad place where you could be up to a week trying to get through, if you ever got through! It's very tough going. You could also go through the Mediterranean, but captains would not do that because it cost money through the Suez Canal."

He stopped and allowed me to think about it, then continued, "The captain had to decide and plan his course before he left because if he did not know where he was going then we could end up anywhere. So Joe you have to plan."

He sat back, and then added perhaps the most important part. "But, Joe," he continued. "Once you have your plan, you have got to believe in it. Believe in it and it will surely happen the way you planned."

We sat for a while in the woods, just listening to the sounds of summer and life and said nothing.

"Uncle Andrew," I said. "Will there be many fish there in a week?"

"I hope so, Joe," he replied as he looked into the water and at our sheep's head.

We stood up, slowly walked back down the track and got on the bike. I sat on the cross bar and we went home.

A week later we were back in the woods and all that was left of the sheep's head was the scull still hanging by the wire from the tree.

"Well Joe," said Uncle Andrew. "Let's see what we can

catch." We set up the rods and got it all ready. We were fishing with very small hooks with no weights at all on the line. We were using live maggots that Uncle Andrew grew and they were in some sawdust in a little tin box. Uncle Andrew put one on a hook. It was late in the evening, about 8 p.m. when we started fishing, just the right time for the trout to feed.

Uncle Andrew let the line float down the river and he had one on his line as soon as it got to the pool by the bend in the river. I also had one within a minute. My fish was just under a pound and so was Uncle Andrew's. We caught a total of seventeen fish in the space of an hour.

"This is what I call fishing," I said to Uncle Andrew. It was now getting dusk and time to go home with our bag of fish.

"See what planning can do for you Joe?" said Uncle Andrew. "Always plan ahead." He had a big smile on his face as he said, "Plan my boy, plan."

I never forgot those words of advice or the practical way Uncle Andrew proved them to me and I have used them in nearly every aspect of my life since. Uncle Andrew knew the value of those words and he gave me something to guide me through my years. What a wonderful Uncle I had and what a wonderful lesson in planning I had received. One that was to last me all of my life.

The other great fishing lesson was in May and June. This was another natural event of which Uncle Andrew took advantage. It was the time of the Mayfly and the Woodfly.

He said the trout love these flies especially the Woodfly.

Uncle Andrew had a cow horn with a piece of metal over the wide end of the horn with very small holes in it. At the narrow end was a small cork. The cow horn must have seen many years of service for this is where he kept the flies. First of all we had to catch them. Uncle Andrew had his own methods for catching them.

We would climb over the stall next to the gate at the dam and cross the field near the wood. We were looking for cow droppings and we always found some. The sun had usually baked the surface hard so we used a stick and opened it up to the moist dung inside. We did this at three dung heaps and sure enough the flies appeared.

For his age, Uncle Andrew was very quick with his reflexes. We would wait by the dung heap and the flies would land on the cow pat. We had to pass our hand very quickly over the pat and catch the flies. We would normally catch one or two. We would put them in the cow horn and you would hear them buzzing inside. When we had enough we would start putting the rods together and start fishing. This was a different kind of fishing to that where we had to get the artificial flies to behave as though alive.

When I watched Uncle Andrew baiting his hook, I noticed something strange. "Uncle Andrew," I asked. "Why do you put two flies, one on top of another, on the hook?" I said.

"Well Joe," he replied. "It's like this. The Woodflys get up in the trees over there, above the water, and start mating. They get a bit excited and forget about the water and fall in. The trout are waiting below to have dinner."

We started at the tree line. Uncle Andrew put my flies on for me and I cast it into the slow running water.

"Just walk along with it Joe," advised Uncle Andrew. "But stay away from the bank, because the trout can see you. And don't talk. Stay very quiet as you go along."

I went down the river toward the dam and sure enough I caught one just before the sluice gate. Uncle Andrew caught four and was again very happy. When we got home Willie was there and he always cooked the fish. For a reason I could never discover, Auntie May refused to cook fish.

"Riley. How many did you catch?" asked Willie.

"I caught one," I answered. "That big one there, just near the sluice gate."

"Well done, Boyyo," said Willie.

The frying pan was out and we were all ready for the fish. Willie gutted them and then rolled them in flour, then fried them in the pan. They tasted so good.

During the winter nights, Uncle Andrew and Sean would be seen at the table making different flies. They were so delicate and so colourful. Uncle Andrew used to put one or two flies in paraffin oil.

"Why do you do that, Uncle Andrew?" I asked.

"Oil floats on water Joe" he replied. "So I put them in the paraffin oil so they will not sink. The oil coats the fly and it floats. It works well in the lakes but not so good in a fast flowing river."

Uncle Andrew had a box full of the most magnificent flies you have ever seen and they were all put to good use.

That was my Uncle Andrew. A patient teacher; a kind and gentle man, always ready to pass on his wisdom, my mentor who remains to this day, my hero.

CHAPTER NINE

Scoutmaster Willie

By now, you will have read about Auntie May, Uncle Andrew, Gerard and Sean, and you must be getting the impression that I had died and landed amongst angels. To me, they were angels, but the next son, Willie, was not only an angel to me, but to the whole town of Kilrush.

When he was about eighteen years of age, Willie worked for The Bank of Ireland as a bank messenger and earned about 12 shillings a week. From that he would pay everything to Auntie May who then returned to him his usual pocket money. Willie would gripe about the amount every week as he always needed a few bob more.

Willie was fastidious about his appearance. He was always well dressed, his shirts were ironed and starched, shoes polished, creases in his trousers and not a hair out of place. The Brylcreem kid, as I called him. He was totally opposite to others in the family as he was outgoing, sociable and a very happy, chatty guy. This made him a popular figure with the entire townsfolk.

Willie was only about 5 feet 6 inches tall. He had a fair complexion with brown hair with a body veering towards tubby. He had a good voice and loved to sing. So much so,

Willie was a member of the operatic society that Kilrush had at that time. The operatic society would put on one big show every year at the Mars Cinema. One year it was The Desert Song, the following year the Student Prince. They brought a famous lady opera singer from England to play the major role in the Desert Song. Even today, I can remember her name—Elizabeth Flood.

Willie was responsible for so many things happening in Kilrush. Everything he did for the community was, for him, a labour of love.

Willie was very religious in his ways. He never missed mass or retreat and every Sunday would see him attending the evening service at the church. He was like a brother and a father to me and I was so lucky to have such an example in my life. Every night when we went to bed, Willie would get me to kneel with him beside the bed and he would lead us in prayers.

Willie wanted to help people, especially those less fortunate than himself. He neither sought nor received anything for his efforts.

He alone was responsible for giving hundreds of boys in Kilrush the opportunity to join the Boy Scouts.

He formed the Boy Scouts in 1951 with the help of his brothers Sean and Gerard. I remember when the Scout books arrived and the brochure with all the different photographs of uniforms in them.

This became a family project in a way, as we were all in the kitchen and Willie had the books out on the table. It came to the uniform side of things and what type of uniform should we have.

Katie was the authority on dress and material. There was a lot of discussion on the subject. Johnny Enright, a suitor of Katie, liked the old style hat with the wide brim. Katie said they are not practical with the winds we had in Kilrush.

Sean liked the khaki colour uniform while Gerard preferred the navy blue.

It was eventually decided that we would have the navy uniform with the beret. This was adopted and shirts, berets, etc. were ordered from Dublin and arrived some weeks later. My only claim to fame in all of this was I was the first boy in Kilrush to put on the Boy Scout uniform - because I was used as the model.

The boxes arrived and were opened up. The shirts and trousers were laid out on the table with the badges etc.

"Riley. Come here," said Willie

Katie held a number of shirts against my chest to find one that would fit.

"Get in the parlour and try them on," ordered Willie.

I put on the uniform and came out into the kitchen. They put a beret on my head and that was it, the decision had been made, I was wearing what the future Boy Scouts of Kilrush would consider their uniform.

Willie had already recruited his senior boys. The patrol leaders were Senan Shalloe, Senan Halpin, Joe Moody and Pat Galvin. Pat Galvin proved to be a very wise choice, as not only did he go on to lead the band, but later in life devoted a great deal of time and effort to the Scouting movement. He and Willie were to share not only the same visions, but a deep friendship that lasted all of Willie's life. Pat Galvin was yet another unsung hero of Kilrush.

These were to be the core of the Kilrush Scouts along with the important role of bugler, which went to Richard Doyle. They were the first boys to take the Boy Scouts oath in the Christian Brothers School with their parents watching on.

I became a Boy Scout in the second wave made up mostly of the scallywags, like John Doyle, Joe Flynn, Senan Corbett, Ken Humphries, Paddy Enright and a lot of others from all around the town.

However, I did go on one of the first camping expeditions to Kilkee, an event that I am sure will bring back memories for those who were there.

We got the West Clare train from Kilrush to Kilkee. We borrowed a big handcart from the railway station and it was loaded up at our house on the Friday afternoon.

We loaded the only big bell tent that we had onto the train and off we went on the first adventure for the Scouts of Kilrush.

We arrived at Kilkee and borrowed the station cart. We loaded it with everything including our food and off we went. We passed along the front by the beach and turned left toward the Carrigaholt Road. Willie had received permission to put us in a field there, just on the edge of the town. We were all so excited. I should have not been there because this was for the senior boys only. Senan Shalloe took objection to my being there at all, and let me know about it on a few occasions.

Our first job was to put up the tent and some of us were sent to find some wood for the fire. We had no ground sheet for the bell tent and it was decided that we would do a Paddy Griffin and "borrow" some hay from the farmer's field next to ours. It was now becoming dark and Senan Shalloe was to head the sortie into the farmer's field for the hay. Off they went, three of them lying low as they crept along the wall, eventually hopping over the wall into the field. When they got back they did not have enough to cover the ground so they had to go back again. Willie could not condone this action so he sat by the camp fire and pretended that nothing was happening.

The boys were back in about 15 minutes, this time with a lot more hay. Travelling both to and from the haystack, the three of them crouched low, moving from one hiding place to another as though they were an attacking army. The irony of it all was there was not a house or a person within a mile of us. The only one's that saw us were a few cows, a horse and a donkey. The boys left a trail of hay across two fields. The farmer would not have had to be a genius to trace where his hay had gone.

Willie supervised the cooking and we had a great meal. Willie was the only one of the boys that Auntie May had taught to cook. We sat around the campfire and the boys talked about what other activities should be planned for the summer.

You could tell from where Willie had received his ability to plan. In years gone by, doubtless Uncle Andrew had given his talk on planning to Willie, and it had sunk in.

Soon, it was time for us to bed down in the tent. Camping or not, Willie still donned his usual striped pyjamas. I never remember him ever going to bed without wearing his striped pyjamas.

We all got into the tent and there were a few jokes while Willie turned out the oil lamp. There was much laughter in the dark with the odd joke thrown in here and there.

The next thing I knew Willie was complaining something terrible.

"Come on," said Willie. "Who let off?"

Nobody answered his question, we just laid there laughing.

"Oh my God," said Willie. "That's terrible." We could hear him stand up, and then the lamp came on in the tent as Willie stood at the open flap. "I don't know who that is, but you should see a doctor."

Willie went outside and then we all noticed the smell and it was really awful. Senan Shalloe had a different, but more direct question. "Who the fok farted?" he asked.

Outside, Willie was complaining because the bottoms of his pyjamas were getting wet from the dew on the grass and his feet were cold. By now the evacuation of the tent had become a mass exodus.

We all ended up outside the tent accept for one Richard Doyle. I am not accusing Richard of this dastardly deed, but I think he would have a hard time convincing the others that he was not the culprit.

All in all it was a great weekend and achieved what Willie wanted, which was to create a team of senior boys and plan out the rest of the summer. We went home on the Sunday on the West Clare railway.

Willie, although a great deal of fun, if he felt our behaviour was outside of the honour of the Scouting movement, could be very strict.

A good example of this was his policing of our visit to Mars Cinema. On this particular Saturday afternoon when we were about 13 years of age, a group of us, all Scouts, decided to take our girlfriends of the time to Mars Cinema. Although we were too innocent to know why, we did know that it was very grown up when with your girlfriend to sit in the back row. It was quite a group of us that day. There was Richard Doyle sat next to Dympna O'Leary, John Doyle with Claire Moody, Senan Corbett with Breda Carmody and myself with Patricia Carmody. Ken Humphries and a few others made up the group.

We were all rapt in the picture when someone came through the door and shouted, "Willie is coming."

The brave Boy Scouts forgot about protecting their fair maidens, just jumped out of their seats and scattered. I ran down the stairs to the balcony front then jumped the rail, knowing it was not far to the floor. I was grabbed by Gander Daly, a six-foot man, who marched me to the back and threw me through the door into the lobby.

Willie was waiting for us outside in the lobby. I was one of the last to be thrown through the door while Senan and Paddy, who stayed upstairs, did not get caught. Willie had John Doyle, Richard, Ken Humphries and the rest of us stand to attention while he lectured us. Then he instructed us to attend the troop meeting at the school on the following morning.

On the following morning, a Sunday, he called the whole troop to attention and delivered a stinging lecture on the virtues of Scouts and how Boy Scouts should behave. After we had been called to stand easy, I thought the incident had been forgotten. To my horror, Willie then announced that three of the Scouting Committee, Joe Flynn's father, Tom Soffe and Father Ryan, were sat in the next room to hear our cases. We were being given the Scout equivalent of a court marshal.

Richard Doyle, being the eldest as well as troop bugler, was the first to be marched in. I was second. The charge was that I had been sitting in the back row of Mars Cinema with a girl. I had to plead guilty and was sentenced to two months probation together with a warning of the dire consequences if caught repeating the offence.

My punishment was in reality worse than the others. I lived with Willie and everyday for the next week received a real crack across the ear.

I look back at those beautiful times and I think that Father Ryan, Mr. Flynn, Tom and Willie would have had a good laugh about it behind our backs.

One unusual Boy Scout was Jerome Finucane. Jerome was a real likely lad and we got on so well. Maybe it was because we were both handicapped in a way. Jerome had polio as a child and did not have the use of his legs, however his enthusiasm for life made up for any disability he may have suffered. He had a way with the Kilrush version of the English language that was unequalled by anyone in the town. He matched it with a great sense of humour, which made a so called "crippled person" the centre of many a social occasion.

His wheel chair was a 3-wheeler affair and Jerome had to peddle it by hand. Jerome, John Doyle, Senan Corbett and I had all joined the scouts together. It was great when we went to Mass as a troop as we had no problems at all getting Jerome into church. All the scouts lifted Jerome and the wheelchair up the steps outside. Jerome was our comedian and in a way he helped pull us together. He was always laughing, joking and of course cursing.

John Doyle and I would often go out with Jerome. Many a times we would go out to Cappagh together and as we came to the fort hill Jerome would shout, "Fok you, Riley. Will you push the fokking thing?"

"For fok sake, Jerome," I would reply. "I am fokkin pushing."

"Then Doyle," he would shout. "What the fok are you doing?"

"Would you fok off," answered John. "I am fokking pushing."

When we eventually got to the top we would all hop on board and ride down the hill again. We once had a bad accident near Moody's Shop opposite the National School. We had been up to Jerome's house and on our way down John Doyle and myself had climbed onto the chair. We got up a bit too much speed coming down the hill. Jerome lost control and we took a real tumble. We all ended up in the road and Jerome was cursing and cut. His mother went mad, his wheel chair was broken and not for the first time. John and I went nowhere near his mother for about a month.

The Scout movement went on for many, many years and these boys were the corner stone of the movement. To all of you I say you have a right to be proud of your achievements because Willie was so proud of all of you and it was plain to see the pride in his eyes, his face and his smile. It gave him so much happiness to see joy in others.

Whenever he came home from a parade he would tell Auntie May all about the boys and how well they marched. With no financial help and no funds this man, Willie

Deloughery, formed the Boy Scouts of Kilrush. For the next twenty years, he helped young people of the town, gave them direction and helped them into adulthood. I do not know one single boy in the town of Kilrush that did not respect and admire him.

He influenced our young lives with his laughter and his sense of humour. He led by example, an example that was hard to match. His patience with the young, his manner, his way of dealing with people, his quiet way, his method of "getting the job done" and getting others to also do it, was a joy to behold.

He got respect not because he commanded it but because he earned it, not only from the Boy Scouts of that time, but the whole community. All of the equipment needed by the Scouts was purchased from the money raised by him running the weekly Bingo session.

He practically single-handed put the graveyard at Old Shanakyle back to some semblance of normality. It had been neglected, overrun with weeds, and was in a terrible state of repair. Many of the tombs and graves there were over one hundred years old and the land was boggy. Willie set about restoring the graveyard to a place of tidiness, peace, calm and reflection. That his good work lead to the graveyard being kept so well ever since, in many ways, is a tribute to his efforts.

His greatest achievement though, that together with his brothers and some friends, he built St. Senan's Well as an act of remembrance of his murdered brother, and in doing so, left the community of Kilrush with a beautiful monument. In all of these efforts Willie Deloughery never sought or asked for anything.

He was a true son of Ireland and Kilrush. He loved his home, his family, his town—but most of all its people. He was a person who was held in high esteem, not only then but even today. You would not have to go far in the streets of

Kilrush even today, to find admirers of this great man.

He left an indelible mark on me. May he be helping God in looking after heaven.

Chapter Ten

Footing The Turf

Life was not all motorbike rides and fishing. When it came to surviving, the whole family had to chip in. One of the essential things for survival in Kilrush was to have an ample stock of dried turf. Turf is the Irish term for peat, which remained until recently as the basic solid fuel utilised all over Ireland. In pre-electric days, whether in an open grate or the more sophisticated kitchen range, a supply of dried turf was needed all year round. Over the smouldering turf fire, meals were cooked, kettles were boiled, bread was baked and in the winter, people would gather close around to beat the fierce chill of the winter winds.

During the long summer season, every male in the house assisted in the extraction of turf from the bog. In late spring, Uncle Andrew would seek out where he believed was a suitable location in the bog, then rent it from the owner of the land. Usually he would select a site way up the Kilkee Road, near to Moyasta.

At the onset of summer our horse would be tethered to the cart and Uncle Andrew and I would drive to the site. Upon arrival I would take the cart to the marsh where good grass was available, unhitch the horse, and then tether it on a long rope to the cart.

While I was doing this, Uncle Andrew would be marking out the area he had rented. The first backbreaking task was to clear off the topsoil and expose the compressed turf below. Then, a single trench had to be dug along one edge of the plot. The turf from this was virtually useless, as it did not have the desired oblong shape that would allow it to be stacked for drying.

Once the initial trench was dug we could use the sleán, (pronounced schlawn). The sleán was a flat spade but with one side turned outwards at right angles to the spade face. By progressively moving along the edge of the trench, the sleán would accurately cut out the turf not only in one movement, but with consistency of size.

The sods of turf were heavy with water, so initially each would be laid out over the ground to drain. The sods would be turned over a few days after cutting to ensure drainage was complete. It would then be my job to gather the sods and stack them into ricks. The never-ending winds would blow through the ricks and complete the drying process.

The one unforgettable thing about the bog was the quietness of it all. Uncle Andrew and I would stop on the odd occasion and enjoy listening to the larks singing. Like a lot of western Ireland, the bog was a barren place devoid of trees, just heather and gorse grass. Even what was a gentle breeze in Kilrush would seem gale-force over the bog.

There was nothing to stop the wind or rain once it started and nowhere to shelter. When we had a rain shower, Uncle Andrew and I would sit under the cart and wait for it to pass. The wind-blown rain would slant at an angle that made it almost impossible not to get wet.

Every now and then you would see smoke out in the bog; it meant that someone was making the local brew, the famous poteen. The poteen was made from potatoes and a few ingredients of which I am unsure. It looked like water as it was crystal clear, but it was highly potent stuff to drink.

Paddy Griffin always had some in a little flask that he

kept in his jacket pocket. He called it his Holy Water and claimed it was good for his cough. Of course, Paddy Griffin, as always, could explain why the west coast of Ireland was so barren. As he put it:

"Will you get away our dat. Doesn't it tell you in the Holy Book dat God made the whole world in six days, then rested himself on the seventh? Did you not know that it was on the sixth day dat God was working on west Ireland? Well now. The poor man just ran out of time, and that's why the land is so barren."

When we needed a hand to get the turf cut or dried, on Saturdays Willie and Gerard would join us. Lulu used to come sometimes and make a turf fire to boil a kettle for some tea. We would enjoy this while eating thick sandwiches made from Auntie May's home-cured ham between slabs of homemade bread. Somehow you always felt hungry out there in the bog and everything you ate was so good. In my mind, I can taste the soda bread now and smell the turf fire with its beautiful aroma that hung in the air. It used to be the one thing that struck you when you went into an Irish home, the smell of burning turf.

Lulu used to go for a walk and pick blackberries. She would return with a big smile on her face carrying a basket full of berries. We would eat some and she would tell me off for eating too many. By the end of the day we would have cut a lot of turf and laid it out on the bank to dry.

I always thought it was cold in the bog even on a beautiful summer day. The gentle summer breeze had a slight chill in it from the Atlantic Ocean. We had to cut enough turf during the summer to last us through the year. We knew we had achieved this when the large shed in the back garden was totally full. It was essential to bring in the turf before the rains began. So urgent was this that sometime I would have to forsake going to school and spend the time transporting turf.

Once we reached our house, the cart was unloaded by throwing the turf over the front wall into the front garden. It had then to be picked up, carried through the front door, down the passage to the kitchen, out of the kitchen door, then down the back garden to the shed.

When Willie, Sean and Gerard came home and saw the pile in the front garden you would hear the moans and groans. The turf had to be brought in, and if it was raining then it had to be brought in fast. There would be no rest until this backbreaking work was finished.

Once our shed was full we would bring in the surplus and either sell it to our neighbours or sometimes, even transport it to Scattery Island, which was an adventure in itself.

Although the work was hard, it was a bit sad when the task was completed, because it meant that summer was over, the long evenings on the wane and soon, the winter storms would be on us.

CHAPTER ELEVEN

Back To School

All too soon, the summer holidays would be over and we would reluctantly traipse back to school. I was now seven and in my third year. All of us were pleased to discover our new teacher for the year was Mr. Johnny Griffin, the son of Maude Griffin who had the shop just down the road from our house. Maude was the sister of the infamous Paddy, our storyteller. At one time Maude, like many other shops, had a small bar in the corner of her shop. Perhaps to call it a bar is a bit of an exaggeration as the total stock consisted of one barrel of porter with a beer pump. Paddy used to be a regular customer, but he always refused to pay full price for anything in his sister's shop, so perhaps this is why the bar ceased to exist.

One famous story told by film star, Oliver Reed (of Oliver and Gladiators fame), is about Maude. Oliver had a holiday cottage a few miles outside of Kilrush via the Pella Road. Every few days he would visit the town driving a beat-up Land Rover to shop for supplies. The first time he visited the shop of Maude; he ducked down to enter the shop and went to the counter. He purchased a few items and then said, "Oh. Do you have a newspaper?"

Maude, peered at him and asked, "And would you be wantin' today's newspaper or yesterday's newspaper?"

Oliver looked at her a bit strangely and answered, "I

would prefer today's newspaper."

"Well," answered Maude, looking very serious. "If it's today's newspaper you'll be wanting, you'll have to come back tomorrow."

Mr. Griffin though, was a big man, with chunky cheeks. Together with his wife and three children, he lived in the house next to his mother that had a door that allowed direct access to the shop. He was a hard teacher, but a fair one. Fortunately, he was not a Christian Brother, but he was still strict. For some reason, the beatings I tended to receive were for things I did out of school rather than in.

One particular incident was the time I wanted to get out with my friends Sean and Paddy straight ways after school. I knew that if I entered our house, Auntie May would ask me to take Gerard's tea pail to him at the flourmill. To avoid this, when I arrived at our front gate, with a mighty heave I threw my satchel containing my schoolbooks up the path towards the front door, then ran. What I didn't know was that this action was witnessed by Mr. Griffin as he made his own way home.

The next morning, as sure as God made day, he was there with his famous chant, "Riley. Come out here."

I arose out of my chair and walked slowly to the front of the class, still unaware of my crime.

"Now, Riley. Put both of your hands out palms up," intoned Mr. Griffin. He raised his cane and thwacked me three hard strokes on one hand, then followed it with three on the other.

"Riley," he said. "Don't ever be throwing your schoolbooks around again. Now return to your seat."

Putting my hands under my armpits, I mumbled a "Yes, sir," and sat down. My hands stung, but not a tear came from my eyes. I could feel all of the other boys' eyes upon me, but I had learned at an early age never to cry. I had received many savage beating from the Christian Brothers, but I never let the bastards have the satisfaction of seeing me cry.

One fine evening, I had decided to go to Mars Cinema. I was alone, but there was a film I particularly wanted to see. Mars Cinema was located half way along the south side of Frances Street. As previously stated, Frances Street was the second widest street in Ireland outside of O'Connell Street in Dublin.

I emerged from Mars about a quarter to ten. The shortest route home was to cross Frances Street, walk down towards the flourmill until I reached a building that used to be the Bridewell Jail. A lane ran alongside the barracks that led directly to our house.

As Frances Street was deserted, I was crossing this very wide road diagonally when I noticed Brother Lyons, the Brother Superior of our school, emerge from the Monastery, the home of the Christian Brothers, which was located between the flourmill and the house of Mrs. Glynn. Brother Lyons was only a small man who, like Brother Walsh, needed to wear heavy spectacles, but he had a fearsome reputation for his brutality.

Although I wasn't sure that he had seen me, being in the middle of the road meant I had no choice but to continue. It was a beautiful evening, and from where I was I had a fine view of the sun slowly slipping into the sea between the outcrops of the heads.

Brother Lyons kept walking ever closer to me. He was dressed as always in his long, black flowing gown, sporting a half collar. Rosary beads were swinging from his hip, and in front of him he held an open Bible from which he was reading. Although he gave no indication of it, I was sure he had seen me. I passed within ten feet of him, and then rapidly broke into a run, turned out of his sight into the lane and reached home in record time.

The following morning, during one of our lessons, the classroom door was violently slammed open and to the front of the class strode Brother Lyons. He turned and looked at us. "Riley," he shouted. "Out here." It was not without trepidation that I arose and walked towards him. From his hand dangled his favourite weapon, a length of hawthorn branch with many raised knots on it.

I reached him and asked,"What have I done, sir?"

Before I knew what happened, he had hit me a vicious blow with the back of his hand. I went sprawling onto the floor, dazed. That blood was coming from my nose and mouth was confirmed when I wiped the back of my hand across my face. Not content with that, Brother Lyons, with the rage of a madman, picked me up by my collar and shook me like a rag doll.

"You dare question me?" he repeatedly said as he shook me. "Now, hold out your hands."

I stood there as he raised his stick and applied the downward stroke with all of his might. The pain of each blow was almost unbearable. Eight times the stick descended, but there was no way the bastard was going to see me cry. I think that he had put so much effort into those eight blows that he had no energy to hit me anymore. When he stopped, he shoved his sweaty little face into mine and shouted, "Riley. If I catch you out at that time of night again, I will put you in Borstal." With that, he turned and left the room. Could Borstal be any worse than being in a school administered by him and his fellow Christian Brothers? He was a bombastic bastard of inhumanity who profaned to be a religious representative of God and a religious man, someone to be revered in society. My God, what an example of religious fervour and brutality this sod was. For ever after, to me the flowing robes and rosary of the Christian Brothers would represent the standard uniform of a sadistic bastard.

After he had left, Mr. Griffin led me outside to the water tap and cleaned me up. Mr. Griffin never said a word while he was doing this, but I could see in his face that he had been shocked by the brutality against a seven-year-old that he had witnessed.

Perhaps the only good thing about school was the chance to make new friends. One of my best friends was Mike Melican whose father was the green keeper at the Kilrush Golf Club, just out of town. His father was originally a Scattery Island man.

Michael's house was a small thatched roofed cottage set on the edge of the golf course near the road. This cottage had three rooms; a kitchen in the middle, a bedroom at one end and at the other end there was a partition that went half-way up to the ceiling. It was in this third section they kept the horse, a cow and a few chickens. The chickens always seemed to wander around the kitchen. The girls would sleep in the bedroom while Michael and his parents slept in the kitchen. The place was warm and snug as it had one of those very big fireplaces where the pot hung on a steel arm that swung across the fire. One could sit in the corner of the fireplace it was so big.

There was no running water in houses in the country. Water had to be drawn from a well in the backyard using a hand pump. There was an outdoor privy, a rough affair. It was well away from the house and painted green to blend in with the foliage that surrounded it. Mrs. Melican would always give us milk to drink and some of her still-warm homemade bread. The milk was always served in a cup as they could not afford glasses.

In the field opposite Mike's house was a large fairy ring. A fairy ring was easily recognizable. It was a circle of raised earth. Legend had it that if you trod on or in the fairy ring, then you were cursed for life. Mike and I once crept into that field to look at it from a distance, after which we never ever dared go into the field again. Even though I have since learned that the ring is probably the foundation of an early dwelling, I admit I still wouldn't go near one.

CHAPTER TWELVE

The Story Of St. Senan's Well

This is a story that has to be told as I'm sure the people of Kilrush have no idea of how their beautiful monument at St. Senan's Blessed Well came to be erected.

St. Senan's Well is situated in what was then known as the Convent Fields. Today, if you take the road to Kilkee that rises steeply out of Kilrush, at the top of the hill there is a sign on the left inscribed, "The Blessed Well". Back in the late 1940s no monument existed. The well had just a few stones around it; that was all. As boys we used to play in the hilly fields at the back of our house and that's where St. Senan's Well was located.

The story behind the well is that St. Senan arrived in Kilrush and rested on this spot. It is said that St. Senan was thirsty so he struck the ground with his staff and water came from it. That allegedly happened 1500 years ago and the well is preserved today only because of the love of four brothers. The brothers were Gerard, Willie, Sean and Andrew Deloughery.

Their younger brother, Joseph, had been only 17 years of age when he was beaten to death at St. Senan's Well on the 17th March 1944. This murder still remains today an unsolved crime.

A beautiful monument now stands at the well. The

people of Kilrush believe it is a monument to St. Senan, but that is not strictly true. This is a monument built to the memory of a lost brother, built with love and tears. So much passion went into every brick and every piece of concrete.

The brothers put together whatever money they had to purchase materials for that monument. Gerard was saving to buy a motorbike, but every penny was donated willingly to the project. They sold the horse and cart and curtailed all unnecessary spending in order to raise the not inconsiderable amount required.

They started building this project about 1948. Every day, after work, the brothers would walk up to the well and start clearing the area. Using just shovels, their first task was to clear the ground, then excavate a fair portion of the hillside in order to create a level foundation for the monument. It was hard, backbreaking work.

Although I had no idea what they were doing I contributed by going home to fetch the can of hot tea and some bread that Auntie May would prepare for them. I would return across the fields to the site and the boys would sit on the grass and have tea.

After a while, when the site was ready, came the time that a lot of materials were needed to be taken to the well. The lane that led to it was uphill and always boggy, even in summer. At this time we had no horse or cart so Jack Morrisey came to the rescue with his donkey and cart. Jack was a big man and had lost one of his hands. He had substituted this lost hand with a steel hook. Jack was a kind man. He would let me help him harness the donkey to the cart, and then I would drive it to pick up Willie. We would then go to the builder's yard in the Square where Gerard's good friend, Mike O'Gorman worked. We would load the cart with sand, cement and some blocks. We would then slowly but surely come down past Christian Brothers School, past the handball alley and up the lane next to Jack Morrisey's house. About a mile up the lane we would reach the Blessed Well. Gerard and Sean would have been busy preparing the ground for the foundations.

One must remember that these men were not educated in the building trade. They were not bricklayers or carpenters.

Willie's outgoing and friendly ways meant that there were few people in Kilrush that he didn't know. One of these was an architect, and the brothers paid him to provide the design for the monument they wanted to build. The design called for a top structure that could only be made by a certain company in Limerick. The brothers had placed their order for this.

The driving force behind the building of this monument was a mixture of true emotions, the love, the grief and the sorrow that these boys felt for their dead brother.

There were other regular helpers in this project such as their great friends Johnny Enright, Pat Galvin and Joe O'Donnell. They were all around the same age. Pat you know of from the scout movement. Johnny was a big man with a red round face that was always smiling. If something needed to be moved that appeared immovable you could bet your life that Johnny would move it. He was as strong as an ox and on many occasions when they were digging out the foundations when they came across some large stones and rocks, Johnny would sort it out. Most of the time the work was carried out in a solemn silence, however every now and then they would be times when laughter would be heard and it was usually Johnny's laughter that would carry across the fields.

Joe O'Donnell was a handsome young man with black curly hair, the lady-killer of the district. Joe was a great dancer and had a twinkle in his eye for all the young ladies in the town. He was definitely one for the priests to keep an eye on! Joe was also a good singer. Willie and Joe were great friends and would often attend the dances and other social gatherings together.

Digging out the foundations was very hard; the boys had to dig out tons of soil, rocks and stones. It was always wet under foot because the water seeped out of the side of the hill into whatever they had dug out. All of these people had full-time jobs. Gerard as an engineer in the mill, Sean as the engineer on the boat, Joe O'Donnell worked at Doherty's wood yard, Johnny worked at the creamery and Willie worked as a messenger for the bank. Sean at this time was working on the boats between Kilrush and Limerick and spent as much time on the project as he could when he was home. However Willie and Gerard would go up to the well each evening after tea with Senan Corbett and me tagging along.

Sometimes Joe would go along in the evening but it was harder for Johnny to go at that time. He had to start so early in the mornings, before the farmers arrived with their milk. However he never missed a weekend.

It took them about six months of really backbreaking work and all of this work was done in there own time and all by hand. The money for the project came from their own pockets and they never asked anyone in the town for a penny.

Nearly everything that was brought to that well was brought by Jack Morrisey's donkey and cart or occasionally, especially towards the end of the project, the horse and cart of Jack Hanrahan, as it was bigger.

Gerard borrowed one of the trucks from the mill to go to Limerick to pick up the top sections. They left very early in the morning while I was still asleep. When I discovered they had gone, I got very upset because they did not take me.

A lot of the road was unmade over the 20 miles from Ennis to Kilrush. It would have been slow driving on the way back with their very precious cargo as this had to be delivered intact and in one piece.

The sections were delivered and, as the truck could not traverse the lane, were put against the side of the house of Jack Morrisey. It took about eight men to get them unloaded from Glynn's truck.

The sections looked very big to me and they were very heavy. When they took the first section up the lane to the well, they filled sacks with hay and put them on Jack's cart. It was not an easy journey to the site because of the weight of each section. I was too small to help and would only get in the way. The boys had to help the horse and push the cart up this boggy lane, across the field and down to the well. It took about eight of them to lift each delivered section off the cart and lay it on the ground. My job was to open and close the gates along the way.

This was repeated another four times and at the end of the afternoon the brothers, Johnny Enright, Joe O'Donnell, Jack Hanrahan and Jim Morrisey were exhausted from this backbreaking work

They built the foundation with such loving care because everything had to be right. Willie would mix the cement and sand while I would fetch the water. If you go to the well today you would appreciate the mammoth efforts put in by these people building this monument. Everything that is there at that well was brought by horse and cart or donkey and cart, the ground was dug with a loving care, the cement was all mixed by hand with the odd tear in it here and there.

Willie, Gerard and Sean went to see the Canon because in the church was a statue of St. Senan. It was a beautiful statue and it was in the main knave of the St. Senan's Church. They went to the Canon and asked permission to relocate the statue of St. Senan from the church to the well. This was done before the plans were drawn up to allow the statue to be incorporated in the design. The Canon was shown the plans and gave permission for the statue to be removed from the church and to be taken to the Blessed

Well by the brothers. Once permission had been granted, the statue of St. Senan was measured and the structure built to accommodate it.

That evening when we took the statue from the church I thought how appropriate it was that an ass would take St. Senan to the well because Jesus Christ had entered Jerusalem on one. If it was good enough for Jesus Christ it was certainly good enough for our saint.

Unfortunately, the statue was too big to put on the cart as the donkey got in the way. We could not balance the statue correctly. We had to go to the mill and get a large handcart.

We filled bags with hay and straw and placed them on the cart to act as a cushion for our Saint to rest on during his journey.

When you walked into the church, the statue of St. Senan was on the left-hand side on a seven-foot high shelf. The boys with the help of two ladders and quite a few people lifted the statue down very carefully because this statue was life size. Like a coffin they carried St. Senan out of the church on their shoulders and laid it on the cart.

This was the start of the journey of St. Senan to the Blessed Well and for those people of the town of Kilrush who may wonder how St. Senan got to the well, here is the story.

It was a beautiful Saturday afternoon. On the following day the monument was going to be consecrated so everything had to be in order and finished.

We left the church at about five o'clock. The sun was shining and for once there was no breeze. It was a beautiful evening. St. Senan was placed on the cart and of course the working faithful were all there, Gerard, Sean, Willie, Johnny and Joe O'Donnell. A few other people were also there either to watch on or give assistance. The statue was carried out of the church by the boys and placed on the waiting cart with

Johnny and Joe and a couple of other people to help because the statue was heavy and also fragile.

The statue was placed on the cart and we proceeded towards Pound Street, past the school, past the convent and the handball alley. Then off we went up the lane by Jack Morrisey's house.

All of this was done by man's sweat alone, there being no cranes, tractors or implements to dig, or anything else mechanical. Everything concerning the construction of the monument was done with love, with passion and by hand.

It took about an hour to get the statue to the site because it was slow going in the mud and on the rough road. When we got it there it had to be put into place. If you stand at the front of the monument you can look up at the magnificent statue and wonder how we got it there in that day and age.

At the back of the well they placed planks of wood on the ground to the top section and slowly but surely, and may I add with a lot of cursing, the statue was put in place. We stood back in amazement and looked at it and the sight was beyond the expectations of any of us. Here was St. Senan as never seen before in all his glory, it was as if he had waited all those years to come home.

Father Ryan was there to make sure that all went well and I think he closed his ears to the odd slip of the tongue, as did St. Senan. The last thing to go into place was the glass. The glass was specially made for the monument. By the time it was all finished it was about 9:30 p.m. and the only thing left to do was for Willie to go up the ladder to clean the glass.

On the Sunday it was announced at all Masses that St. Senan's Well was to be consecrated. The well, prior to this time, had never been consecrated. The history of how it came to be had been handed down through the centuries.

After the midday Mass a lot of people went to the well.

The priests were there including Father Ryan, who later did the consecration, together with the Christian Brothers and the nuns.

The people stood on the hillside as you came down from the Kilkee Road and there were lots of people around the Well itself. It was a solemn occasion for the brothers as well as Johnny and Joe. Here were ordinary people who performed an extraordinary feat that I believe equivalent to that of any building anywhere on this planet. One thing is for sure. There is not one structure on this planet that received so much love, so much care as this structure had. It was built out of the love of a lost brother and I believe that it is a monument not to St. Senan but to the family who built it, the Deloughry family.

If you live in or visit Kilrush, go to this very solemn place and look at this simple but very beautiful monument. Remember the story of the people who placed it there and why it was built. It was built because it was the right and only thing to do by these young men who loved their brother. Remember too the harshness of those times and the poverty that they endured, with very little money but a lot of love, dedication and energy they built a shrine of magnificence that would last hundreds of years.

The Blessed Well holds so many very special memories and to those who now read this story and go there, they will see this monument in all its glory and perhaps feel the love and pain that went into its construction. To those people mentioned and their families, I say, be proud of those very religious and dedicated people.

The shame of it all was neither Auntie May or Uncle Andrew ever went near the place, for the pain they felt for the loss of their son, Joseph, was too much to bear.

Chapter Thirteen

Paddy Griffin

Perhaps the only memorial to Paddy Griffin will be these next few pages. This is very sad, as Paddy deserves better. For a growing boy, with the exception of school, living as I did in Kilrush was fantastic. The cream upon my cake, however, was Paddy Griffin. His ability to hold all of us spellbound with his many scary stories. To make us laugh at his outrageous claims, and his ability to win any argument with illogical logic is unforgettable. His outwardly scruffy appearance belied what must have been possession of a highly intelligent brain. He could come up with an original story at the snap of a finger.

Although everybody knew Paddy Griffin and had heard his stories and jokes, because of his long-time friendship with Uncle Andrew and the many years they had served together in the Royal Navy, I was fortunate to be exposed to his wit more than most.

During the summer months, night time arrived almost at the same time as bedtime. There was so much to do in Kilrush that we were rarely indoors until dark.

The winters, however, were quite a different story. In winter, darkness descended early. There were storms with fierce winds slamming into the town from the Atlantic Ocean. Often, the windows would go white with the deposited salt from the sea. In the winter we would gladly all assemble in the kitchen where the glowing turf kept us snug and warm.

Auntie May would be in her usual chair close to the kitchen range. Uncle Andrew, when not making fishing flies, would be in his chair, and in the corner would be Birdie, softly playing magical tunes on one of his many mouth organs. The rest of us would be chatting or reading comics. Very often Johnny Enright and some of the other friends of the brothers would also sit around either gossiping or discussing the issues of the day.

It would not be unusual for Paddy Griffin to drop by on his way home from having a few glasses of porter and a swig from his flask of poteen.

Paddy would reminisce about the past with Uncle Andrew. Sometimes they would be interrupted by a comment from one of the boys and Paddy always had a quick retort.

An example is that one night Willie asked of him, "Paddy. Did you know that Mick Scanlon died in his sleep last night?"

Paddy replied, "I did, and if he wakes up in the morning the shock will kill him."

Paddy Griffin would have been a great hit as an actor. He was the finest teller of stories, especially scary stories that I have ever heard. He made everything so real, changing his voice to accommodate the character. He would include such as, "- and the wa-ai-ai-l of the banshee was right alongside me." After he had finished, we were all scared to go outside. If Cissie Roughan and the two Enright sisters, Joseta and Breda were there, they would all refuse to go home unless one of the boys accompanied them. Cissie only lived about fifty yards away, diagonally opposite us, whereas the Enrights were about 150 yards down Pound Street. The boys used to make fun of them for being afraid, and would escort them. Funny though, when they came back, both would be breathing heavily as though they had been running.

The trouble was that Paddy would set the scene of some of his scariest stories so close to our house. "Wasn't I coming home late one night down near the handball alley, and just before I reached this house, didn't I see the banshee? A terrible sight she looked, starin' at me with those eyes of death. I didn't know what to do. 'Dis is the end,' I thought. Then I pulled out my cough medicine for a last gulp, and I noticed her look change. I suddenly realized that she had an awful thirst on her, so I offered her my flask. And didn't she take it and have a mighty swallow. She returned it to me smiling and said, 'You're all right, Paddy Griffin. There will be no harm coming to you this night,' then she just disappeared."

We believed him, all of us. Such was the power of his storytelling.

Another night, there was a serious discussion taking place about the Bible and the subject came around to Adam.

"For all we know," said Sean. "Adam could have been a Chinaman."

"Will you get away wid our dat," said Paddy. "For sure Adam was not a Chinaman."

"You don't know that, Paddy," said Sean. "He could have been."

"I'm telling you for sure that Adam was no Chinaman," insisted Paddy.

"How can you be so sure?" asked Willie.

"Well now, I'll tell you," commenced Paddy. "Your da' and me, we've sailed all over the world, and we seen many places including China. I'll tell you this," he continued. "Those Chinese are clever people but they like some funny foods. Not for them the tatty. They love rice. They eat many other strange things like bird-nests and sharks fins."

"Away with you," said Sean.

"Tis true enough," said Paddy. "Ask your own father." Uncle Andrew nodded.

"So what has all that got to do with Adam?" asked Willie.

"Well, I'm coming to that," replied Paddy. "Will you not listen, Willie? You can't learn anything while you're talking," admonished Paddy. Willie almost blushed while Paddy continued. "They eat all kinds of strange things, even dogs."

"Away with you," said an astonished Sean once more.

"Tis true," continued Paddy. "But the most favourite thing, the biggest delicacy of all is snake. Your Chinamen love eating snakes. Now then, if Adam was a Chinaman, then it stands to reason that Eve was Chinese as well, doesn't it?"

We all found ourselves nodding our heads in agreement.

"Well then," continued Paddy. "If they were Chinese, sure they would have eaten the snake first."

I looked at Uncle Andrew who had lowered his face so that his expression could not be seen. Gerard just sat at the table, guffawing with the tears coming down his eyes. Sean and Johnny exited along the passage and into the front garden where we could hear their laughter. Willie sat there totally bemused, while I thought the whole thing made sense. Or did it? Paddy just looked at me and winked.

Another time, Willie and Sean were playing darts in the kitchen. Paddy was sitting there talking away to Uncle Andrew.

Willie suddenly said, "Paddy. Will you look at that? A bull's eye."

"Will you away our dat, 'tis nothin'," answered Paddy. "I was the fastest and greatest dart player in the world."

Willie smiled and held out the darts to him. "Come on

Paddy, show us," he said.

"No. Sure I had to give it up," replied Paddy.

"What do you mean, Paddy? You had to give it up," replied Willie.

"I had to give it up," repeated Paddy. "I was playing one night and didn't I have an accident? I used to throw the darts swish, swish, swish, so fast and that the three darts would be in the bull, just like that."

Although he should have known better, Willie walked right into the trap. "What happened to you?" he asked.

"Well," continued Paddy. "This night I threw the darts and they went swish, swish, swish and I was not sure about my first dart.

"So?" asked Willie.

"Well," continued Paddy. "I stepped up to the board to check my first dart," he stopped while he put his hand to the back of his head. "And didn't the other two darts stick into right here in the back of my head?"

Then Paddy just continued his chat with Uncle Andrew as though none of this happened. It took Willie about five minutes to work that one out, but by this time Gerard was doubled over, tears coming down his face with laughter. Willie knew he had been taken in and after a few minutes Paddy gave me a wink and a wry smile as I sat on the floor.

This was not as outrageous as some of his stories. On a Thursday or Friday morning we used to go fishing. This particular day we came back about three in the afternoon. We had a good catch and had caught some really big fish in the waters between Scattery Island and Cappagh.

Paddy had obviously enjoyed a few jars and sat in his usual place behind the door talking about the war with Uncle Andrew.

Our catch included a big bass, a few mackerel and some whiting. Gerard lifted the bass by the tail and held it up for Paddy to see. "Will you look at that, Paddy?" he said. "Caught it off Cappagh pier."

"Will you away our dat. 'Tis nothin' at all," answered Paddy. Then he was away with a story that took all of twenty minutes in the telling.

"I was out there fishing from the pier at Cappagh one day," he began. "I caught this bass and Lord, it was an unmerciful size of a fish."

Gerard nodded, his eyes already glazing over with the rapt attention he always gave one of Paddy Griffin's stories.

"It was so big," continued Paddy, "that although I was playing it for all I was worth, it didn't show any sign of tiring. I had to get a saddle, harness and bit and didn't I ride it up and down the Shannon for three days to tire it out before I could land it? And when I came to land it," continued Paddy. "Didn't it take a team of six horses and a tractor to drag up onto the shore? He was an awful fish to be sure."

Paddy then looked at Gerard. "Would you be knowin' Billy Smart's Circus?" he asked.

Gerard, with a look on his face that showed he knew he was being had, answered, "I do indeed, Paddy."

"Well," continued Paddy. "Didn't I sell the skin of that fish to Billy Smart so that he could use it for a tent?"

"Will you go away yerself," retorted Gerald.

"'Tis true," affirmed Paddy. "And didn't I sell the back-bone to the Liverpool council for them to use as a bridge across the Mersey?"

Not all of his stories were outrageous. Some of them had a ring of truth. Such was the tale he would relate about Con, the barman at Kelly's pub.

"Nothin' at all," he would commence in his normal fashion. "Will you away wid our dat. Did you not hear about the stranger comin' into town and going into Kelly's?. 'Quick, barman, give us a pint of porter, for I've a dreadful thirst on me,' says the stranger. Well, wouldn't you believe that Con just stands there polishing the glasses?," continued Paddy. "Then your man said, 'Did you not hear me? Give me a pint of porter.'

"Well. Con just looked at him," continued Paddy. "Still polishing his glasses, he says, 'I cannot. Sure, it is the Holy Hour, so I can't serve you.'

"The stranger looked at him and said, 'Holy Hour is it? And what time does that run from?' Con told him that it was from 2:30 until 3:30. The stranger turned and looked at the clock behind him. 'But for heavens sake,' the stranger moaned, 'it is only just two minutes past the half hour. Surely you can let me have a pint?' Con carried on just polishing his glasses. 'I'm very sorry,' said Con. 'I'm afraid I cannot.'

"Well, the stranger, didn't he pull up a stool to the bar? 'Then I'll just have to sit here until the Holy Hour ends,' he said.

"Con finished polishing the glass he was holding and put it down. He turned to the stranger and said, 'You're welcome to do that. Would you like a drink while you're waiting?'"

My favourite story, which Paddy always swore as true, was one about himself. Paddy never stole anything in his life, but he borrowed quite a few things that he never got around to returning. He claimed that one day he had almost trod on a magnificent duck. He knew it belonged to the Canon, but he couldn't help himself, he "borrowed" it. Being a Christian man of the faith, he felt bad about it. He waited until he knew that the Canon was taking confession, and then into the church he went to confess. In the confessional box he intoned the usual, "Forgive me father for I have sinned."

"And what is the sin you have committed, my son," replied the Canon.

"Well, I have taken a duck without the owner's knowledge father and want to give it to you," said Paddy.

"I can't take the duck, my son. I don't want it. You must give it back to the owner," stated the Canon.

"I have tried to give it back to the owner," continued Paddy. "But he told me he doesn't want it."

"In that case, my son," answered the Canon. "You can keep the duck and I give you full absolution for your sins."

With a lot of people who can tell a good yarn, you are sure that the same story has been told many times before. Paddy Griffin, however, could instantly come up with a story on such a variety of subjects that I am sure that he was one of those rare people who could think on his feet and blurt out a story to suit the occasion. This was shown one wet and windy day when Johnny, Willie and me returned from the Cricket Field. We had been watching the Clare Championship gaelic football final between Miltown Maibay and the Shamrocks (Kilrush), and unfortunately our lads had been beaten. We were all very depressed. On entering the kitchen, Paddy was sat in his usual chair. Johnny had been bemoaning our loss all the way home, and as we removed our dripping clothes, Paddy asked, "How did the game go, Johnny?"

Johnny went into a long story of the game, how we should never have lost it and by a single goal at that. Once he had finished, Paddy sat back in his chair. "Will you away all dat. Did I ever tell you about the time we were one goal down in the final with 10 seconds to play, but I won the game for them?"

"You played in a final?" and astonished Johnny asked.

"Fetin I did, and I won it," answered Paddy.

"One goal down with only ten seconds to play?" responded Johnny. "And you won? Away with you."

"'Tis true, I tell you," said Paddy. "I was in midfield and I got the ball, I weaved and ducked between five or six players and about 20 yards out from the goal I gave the ball one almighty thunderous kick and didn't it hit the cross bar?"

"And what happened then?" asked a now interested Willie.

"Will hold your wisht. I'm trying to tell you," Paddy said.

"Well, it hit the crossbar so hard, didn't it split the ball into two parts?"

"Go away our dat," exclaimed Johnny, enthralled.

"It's true, the bladder went under the bar and the case went over the bar and remember, we were a goal down," said Paddy.

"So, what did the referee give?" asked Willie.

"Well," continued Paddy. "He had no option but to give me a goal for the bladder under the bar and a point for the case over the bar so we won, by one point."

We forgot about our bad day at the football game and laughed for ages with Paddy and Uncle Andrew. By the sounds of it Uncle Andrew had not heard that one either because the tears ran down his face.

These are but a few of the stories regarding Paddy Griffin. Throughout his life he could bring a smile to anyone's face. When I think of him now, I visualize God sitting there with a smile on his face and Paddy sat at his feet. God is saying, "Get away with you, Paddy. Is that true?" Paddy, may you keep the angels in fits of laughter.

CHAPTER FOURTEEN

Katie's Wedding

I had almost reached the wonderful age of eight, an age where you are no longer considered an infant, but a real boy. It was to be a year of drama, both good and bad. As with all the Deloughery family, Katie was always very kind to me. Katie worked for Mrs. Coffey as a seamstress and Katie made all of my clothes with tender and loving care.

Mrs. Coffey's house was just down the street, opposite the Enright's. Johnny Enright was a big friend of all the Deloughery brothers and spent most winter evenings in our house. Often, the four of them would play cards at the kitchen table. Gerard and Johnny would play partners against Willie and Sean. Willie always seemed to get it wrong and there would be a great deal of fighting going on. With the exception of Sean, none of them smoked or drank.

Virtually everybody in the house knew that Katie and Johnny were courting. The only exception was Auntie May. She loved all of her chickens and seemed determined to keep them all in the coup. She certainly succeeded with the boys, for not one of them was to ever marry. Auntie May had fallen out with Mrs. Enright some time in the distant past. Had she known Katie was courting at all, she would have done everything in her power to stop it. Had she known it was an Enright, even though she really liked Johnny and his sisters, she would have doubled her efforts.

The reason I knew that they were courting was because Katie would use me as an excuse to secretly meet with Johnny. "Tis a warm evening, Joe, will you not take a walk with me for some air?" she would ask. We would walk out to the Cappagh Road and who would we meet but Johnny. I used to eagerly assist in this small deception because Johnny would say, "Joe. Don't tell your Auntie May," and give me sixpence. I kept my end of the bargain, as business was business.

When the inevitable happened, they decided to plan the wedding in great secrecy, fully knowing the storm that would erupt from Auntie May once she knew.

In order to raise the necessary money, Johnny sold the pigs he was raising in his backyard. Sworn to secrecy, my help was solicited in this venture. We used the horse and cart and the side crates that we used for bringing in the turf. Instead of turf, we filled them up with pigs and went to the Square and sold the lot. The famous saying of Katie and Johnny for years to come when asked for a quid was, "we will have to sell the pig".

All in secrecy, the couple had rented a small cottage just down the street from us, and Katie had made her wedding dress, as well as dresses for Mary and Lulu. They had also met with Father Ryan, who knowing the situation and Auntie May's temper, agreed that he would only read the bans for the four consecutive days prior to the wedding, commencing on the Tuesday with the final reading on the morning before the wedding itself.

Come the Monday night before the Saturday wedding, time had therefore run out for Katie. Her mother was bound to hear from one of the neighbours that a ban announcing the wedding had been read out after Mass on Tuesday. As she slept in the same room as Auntie May, Uncle Andrew and the other girls, she left it until we had all gone to bed for the night.

We were all asleep when suddenly a grand commotion woke us all. We could hear Auntie May shouting, swearing and carrying on something awful. We all knew the reason of course. Willie got up and lit the lamp, complaining that they all had to go to work in the morning.

"Jesus, Mary and Joseph," shouted Auntie May. "God almighty in heaven, what has got into the girl?"

Such was the racket, that there was nothing for it but for us all to go down to the kitchen where the fire was stoked and the kettle put on.

Auntie May kept raving at poor Katie, who just sat there crying. Uncle Andrew vainly tried to placate Auntie May, but this seemed to stoke the fires of her anger.

After a couple of hours, Auntie May realized she had been out-manoeuvred, and that whatever she said, Katie was to be wed on Saturday to Johnny Enright. Birdie was the most sensible of us all, as he had stayed in bed and slept all through the storm.

The wedding took place on the Saturday morning and of course we were lucky with the weather. Katie had on a beautiful blue dress that she had made herself.

Everyone was up early. Kaybe and Sue Morrisey came in early and helped out by preparing the wedding breakfast while we were at church for the wedding.

The wedding party assembled, we all walked off to the church. Johnny had to go down the lane and walk up Frances Street with his wedding party because the groom must not set eyes on the bride before the service. Katie was the usual five minutes late.

At the church Johnny was already there with his brothers Stephen, Paddy and Tommy, his sisters Joseta and Breda and of course his mother.

We were all there and the only people missing were

Andrew, who was in Germany and Johnny's father, who was in England.

There were a few other guests like Joe O'Donnell, Jimmy Custy, his brother, Mrs. Coffey and some lads from the creamery where Johnny worked.

I sat next to Auntie May and Uncle Andrew in the second row. Uncle Andrew did his duty, gave his daughter away and walked back down the aisle. He was smiling all the way. So were we all, for Johnny was a nice guy and well known to the family. Katie was so happy.

Willie had, along with the organist, arranged for some of the opera singers to sing.

The wedding party walked back to our house and all was ready for the wedding breakfast.

Johnny and Katie were in the parlour with the best man and bridesmaid. Mary was her bridesmaid and Tommy, Johnny's brother, was his best man.

It was great to see Katie so happy. Katie looked after me like a mum and I loved her so much.

After breakfast they booked Gerard Griffin and went to stay at a friend's house in Limerick for three days on honeymoon.

It was not long before the first arrival. On August 20 a boy named Joseph was born. A year later they had a daughter that they named Mary. These became the closest friends of my life. Joseph and I, later in life, played music together and just enjoyed life to the full.

As well as being a fine musician, Joseph today excels in his chosen profession of teaching in a primary school outside of Dublin, where he has lived since leaving Kilrush. Mary lives not far away from him.

Joseph inherited his musical ability from his father and he may be surprised to hear me say that.

Johnny Enright had a repertoire of songs like you would not believe. He had a fantastic musical memory. He had one problem, though. He couldn't sing. I used to say to him. "Sure didn't God give you the music, but the devil gave you your voice?"

He once took up the banjo and had a great go at "Hey Suzanne" and "She'll be coming round the mountain." Mary and Joseph were only toddlers and loved it. Katie used to look at him with a smile and say, "Lord, Johnny. Will you stop that singing? You're frightening the children."

He always sang with a big smile on his face and at the end he would look at you with an expression that begged the question, "God. Don't you think I'm a great singer?"

Johnny loved all sports, but had a special passion for hurling, Gaelic football and boxing. He started the Kilrush boxing club and used his old thatched cottage down the lane as a club. He did very well and put on boxing shows at the Mars Cinema. He had a ring in the middle of his kitchen and his great prodigy was Senan Shalloe. Senan went on to be the Clare Champion, Munster Champion and all-Ireland finalist.

Another great success, John Doyle, was 6 feet 5 inches tall and a mountain of a man. He was Johnny's heavyweight hope. Unfortunately, when he fought at the Mars Cinema, he got knocked out in the second round.

Johnny would get up at three in the morning to listen to the heavy weight fights on the radio being broadcast from America. Great fights such as Joe Louis and Rocky Marciano against Britain's Don Cockell. He also went to every All-Ireland final and loved it.

All of this disappeared, as he became more involved with his family. The boxing club died when Johnny left it.

Auntie May not only quickly forgot her anger with Katie for marrying Johnny, but also overwhelmed them with her kindness and attention. She insisted that they sit down with us in our house everyday for both dinner and tea. In the evenings, Auntie May would go to Katie's home and together with Girlie Gorman and Maureen Blunnie sit around her fire talking, hardly ever leaving any time for Johnny to be alone with his family.

Johnny still worked hard, and still didn't drink, but he slowly started to change. He would make his way back to his own home after tea, often taking the children with him, but he was unable to shake off the presence of Auntie May. To many people, he just longed to be the master of his own house and family, but Auntie May was not to let go of one of her brood that easy. Without knowing or understanding it, Auntie May was killing him with her kindness.

Perhaps Johnny would have been saved his later life of misery had he taken up golf or some other hobby that induced a private passion. Perhaps had he the courage to seek employment away from Kilrush and insisted on the family joining him he wouldn't have suffered the perceived loneliness that eventually induced him to find solace in a bottle. There is no doubt that Katie loved him with a passion, but was blind to the fact that her husband suffered such pain watching his wife and children being absorbed into the loving amoeba of the Deloughery family instead of them being the Enright's.

Perhaps it is left to the young to see the truth. Johnny Enright died a broken man, but it was nobody's fault. Fate is strange sometimes.

CHAPTER FIFTEEN

Scattery Island

A t the end of another summer, I dreaded the thought of having to start my fourth year at school. I associated school not with learning, but with pain and humiliation. I was to be pleasantly surprised, however, as although the occasional beatings still occurred, I had a certain reprieve. Our new teacher was Brother Gleeson, who discovered something that I had never been aware of, that I was a credible boy soprano and was gifted with an excellent voice. No longer was I sent home when the lesson was religious instruction, but rather instructed to attend and sing solo in church. I probably still hold the record of being the only Protestant to sing Ave Maria in a Catholic Church. I could not be sure, but it occurred to me that St. Patrick would be turning in his grave.

I also sang in all of the St. Patrick Day's concerts. My greatest performance was as the Croppy Boy, a very famous piece of music that is known so well throughout Ireland.

The Croppy Boy was a song about a young Irish Catholic boy who was executed by the British army in Wexford for not informing on the Irish Army and its whereabouts. It was performed complete with a ten-piece orchestra and a twenty-voice chorus. Brother Gleeson conducted and I was the soloist. This musical play was about 30 minutes long.

It gave me a secret pleasure to think about Brother Walsh, the arrogant bigoted bastard that he was and may he turn in his grave, while performing this piece. Here was an English lad performing one of Ireland's most historic pieces of music, and what's more a Protestant to boot.

My God it was great. I had discovered something that I could do very well, better than anyone else in the school, with perhaps the exception of Joe Flynn. Joe was a great singer who I believe let his nerves get the better of him. Once he had left school, Joe turned professional, joining the Black and White Minstrel Show in England. Joe eventually left the glamour of show business and returned to Kilrush to follow in his father's footsteps by becoming a baker.

As a boy soprano I had a hard act to follow. The soprano prior to me was a boy named Joseph Kiely. Joseph was a great singer who went to Dublin and recorded Ave Marie. It was played on the radio for many years, and Joseph was acclaimed as the best boy soprano ever. Joseph was about two years ahead of me in age. When his voice broke a replacement was needed and I fitted the bill.

Because of my singing, the Christian Brothers saw me in a different light and treated me a lot better. I was no longer the outcast Protestant boy that first arrived in school and was persecuted for four years. Not that it mattered so much as my fiery reputation meant that most boys would now leave me alone. I was at last accepted as a local, so much so that a lot of the town's people referred to me as Joe Deloughery.

One of the joys of singing at Mass were the visits, weather permitting, to the congregation on Scattery Island. I had always loved Scattery Island since my first visit to it with Mary Deloughery.

Mary was working for Mrs. Glynn whose family owned the flourmills. Mrs. Glynn was a very kind lady; she never forgot my birthday and always gave me a book. The book would be one of Robert Louis Stevenson's or Charles Dickens classical works. I don't think that I ever really read one completely but did manage to get through most of Treasure Island.

Mary was a great cook and could bake wonderful cakes, which she used to enter local contests. She was very artistic and used to arrange flowers also for the shows. Once we had to take her out to Scattery Island just to pick flowers for an upcoming competition. There were flowers on Scattery Island that could not be found elsewhere. Together with Willie, Gerard, Katie, Joe O'Donnell and Mary, we rowed the three miles to Scattery Island. There were no outboard engines then. As always, I sat up front in the bow. After we had landed on Scattery, Mary wandered through the lanes and fields to find her flowers aided by our inexpert assistance.

Scattery Island is a very historic place. Situated in the mouth of the River Shannon it was attacked many times by the Vikings. The ruins of the churches and some of the houses date back well over a 1000 years. The lighthouse was at the far end of the island and that's where Mary found most of the flowers. Mary had us all picking flowers of different colours and sizes. Once home she would arrange them ready to enter them into the show at the Town Hall.

. Sadly, no one lives on Scattery Island any more. The last family left in 1959, a year after I left Ireland, leaving only a brother and sister to mind the lighthouse. It's sad when you think about it because so many people, including a saint lived on that island for possibly 1500 years.

The Masses on Scattery Island were held on Saturday mornings in the school. I would accompany Father Ryan in the boat. I really enjoyed these weekly outings, mainly because the people on Scattery were so nice. As was the custom, people fasted until they had received Holy Communion, but afterwards, Mrs. McMahon always had a breakfast prepared for us. She lived in a little thatched cottage that she kept very beautiful inside. There, Father Ryan and I would enjoy the eggs, bacon, warm homemade bread and the large cup of tay she provided.

As I grew big enough to handle a currach by myself, I made many Saturday trips to both Scattery Island and Hog Island, exploring them both thoroughly.

These are treacherous waters and one had to know the currents and tides. An out going tide would run at 10 knots between Cappagh and Hog Island and you had better know what you were doing out there in those waters.

On an outgoing tide, I would leave the creek, stay close to shore past the boathouse and along the shoreline to the back of Cappagh pier. I would then hit the current at Cappagh, cross over with the running tide to the end of Hog Island and into the calmer waters between the islands. On an incoming tide I would keep to Scough Point and go towards the heads for about a half a mile. I would then cross the open water from Scough Point to Scattery Island. It would also depend on the wind as to what route I would take and just pray it did not rain along the way. There is no place to hide in those waters.

The island had a small landing area where the water was shallow and very clear. I could not only see the rocks below but also many fish. I would row up to the landing area as this was close to the post office. The post office was a small house with a red iron roof. It had a split door, the top part of the door was always open so you could get attention with the usual saying, "God bless all here."

There was no shop on the island and the closest thing was the post office. You did not go hungry however as someone would always offer you a cup of milk and a piece of home made bread. Some of the boys on the island used to go to our school.

Scattery Island when approached from Hog Island is a wonderful sight. The first thing you notice is the Tower. It is a tall, dark-grey stone tower and overwhelms the skyline, towering over everything in site.

On this island there is a monastery that was built by monks in the 6th century. There were seven churches and St. Senan is reputed to be buried behind one of them. The grave has an old dry stone wall around it, every stone lovingly placed. There is a bar that is across the entrance, set about three feet above the ground. It was said that if you were single and went under the bar you would never marry. I believe that all of the Deloughery brothers had doubted this fable and ducked under it at sometime during their life as not one of them every married.

The tower was built by the monks as a defence from the Vikings who often came to plunder and steal. It had an open door at the base and inside there would have been be a ladder going up for about 50 feet. When the monks saw the Vikings approach they would take their belongings into the tower. When everyone was up in the tower they would then draw up the ladder so the Vikings could not get to them.

A few doors down from the post office stood the most spectacular house on the island, one that is probably a thousand years old. It was a small oval-shaped building having no windows but a hole in the middle of the roof. The walls were stone laid one on another and covered in mud. In places grass and small plants grew on the outside walls.

In the centre of the single room were the remains of what was the fireplace, a round area black in the centre of the floor. It had no windows and the door was very small and arched, it was dark in there with the only light coming through the hole in the roof. I often wondered who would live in such a place. It must have been a hard life on the islands.

Scattery Island is a mile and a half long and half a mile wide. At the far end was the Scattery lighthouse and we never got to know the people who lived there because they would be rotated every so often. The local people themselves, Mrs. McMahon, Mrs. Brennan and their families were fishermen and pilots for the river. Mike Melican who then lived out on the Ennis Road and was the green-keeper for the Kilrush Golf Club, had left the island years before, but he still had some family on the island. I spent a lot of time with the Melican's. Michael, his son, went to school with me.

Large ships would come into the Shannon estuary and heave-to prior to the 60 miles journey to Limerick. The ships would come up the river and lay off Scattery Roads and wait for a pilot to take the ship on to Limerick. You would see these pilots go out to the ships in their currachs from the island. In winter there were some rough waters to contend with but Mike O'Brien's boats were built for these waters.

At the other end of the island was the school for the younger children and that was the part that interested me. At this end of the island, next to the school, was a small inlet and when the tide went out it left behind a large pool of water that sometimes trapped a lot of fish that were easy to catch. I went there one Saturday and to my amazement it was full of salmon. I could not believe my luck. I picked a few good ones and was on my way home sharp. You only ever took enough to eat and give to friends like Mrs. Houlihan, Kaybe or Mrs. Corbett across the road. They really appreciated a good salmon or a bass. You only took enough to feed the family because in those times we had no refrigerators to keep them cold.

I also used to walk between the old church and the tower to the other side of the island looking for mushrooms. Sometimes I would find enough to fill a large bag. Willie used to like the mushrooms done on the open range with some salt sprinkled on them. We would watch as the salt turned to bubbling water on the mushroom and then eat them hot.

Everything had to be brought to the island from the mainland including cattle, food and turf for the fire. We used to earn a bob or two by occasionally taking cattle over. We used to walk them to Ryan's house that was between Cappagh and Aylevaroo. We would do this at low tide, when it was just on the turn. The reason for this was that from there it was only about 200 yards to Hog Island. We would tie the cows around the neck and take two at a time, drag and push them into the water and then row like hell to Hog Island. Once there we would walk the cows to the end of the island closest to Scattery and start all over again, drag them into the water and row to the nearest point of Scattery. We once took a horse, a Grey Connemara. It went crazy on us and tried to get into the back of boat. We decided to keep it in the water the whole way and kept it away from the boat with an oar.

Turf was easy to take over to Scattery. The islanders were always on the look out for a load of turf. I would be walking down Frances Street with a load of turf for sale and one of the islanders would ask you the price. After a fair bargain the question arose as to who was taking it over to the island. They usually did this themselves and I would take the horse and cart down to the creek. I could get a load into a single currach very easily and row it out to the island. If I had to take it over I got an extra half a crown for the effort. It was backbreaking work taking turf out to the island, with no breaks along the way. You just had to keep going.

When we loaded the currach with turf we would commence at the stern and pack the turf up to the bulwark and then we would layer it similarly in the bow. On the bigger boats you could get two loads of turf. Loading and unloading turf is a terrible job as no matter what you did or which way the wind was coming, bits of turf would blow into your eyes.

Hog Island was different to Scattery Island. Scattery

is relatively flat as an island. Hog Island was close to the mainland and had rabbits everywhere. It was used for grazing cattle as it had good grass and spring water. There was only one house on the island and Cody lived there. Cody was in his fifties or sixties, very slim with long grey hair to his shoulders. He would help us when we were taking the cattle to Scattery. He lived on his own and was a hermit.

I don't think anyone knew where he came from and I never knew his last name. He had no family and very few belongings. His clothes were dirty and worn and I think he lived on the wild rabbits that were so abundant on the island.

Cody lived in an old stone house that had mud-covered walls that were two-foot thick. It had a small fireplace and just one small door that was split so the top half of the door could be left open. Although it had a thatched roof, this came very close to the ground, as the external walls were only about four feet high. I suppose it was built very low to withstand the howling gales that came in from the Atlantic in winter. I went into his house once; it was an eerie place. The only light came from the open door and one small window. Cody was all right though as a person. Some people used to tell terrible stories about Cody and none of them were true. They said he was mad and if you went on the island he would kill you, all totally untrue when you met the man. He was a gentle soul and always willing to give you a hand. I can never remember seeing him off the island and it must have been a lonely existence.

CHAPTER SIXTEEN

Tambourine Man

After all he had taught me, I suppose it should have come as no surprise to me that Uncle Andrew was an expert at shark fishing. I suppose I could be forgiven for not being able to link a man who was so skilled at delicately moving an artificial fly in a perfect imitation of a live one, having the sensitivity to know when it had been taken into the mouth of a trout, with the sheer brute strength required in reeling in a shark. But then, Uncle Andrew was always a man of surprises.

Uncle Andrew had an uncanny knack of being able to determine when the times were right for any activity. There was no better person at reading the winds and tides.

On this particular day, he recruited the assistance of Gerard, who had been with him before and had some knowledge of shark fishing. He also recruited Johnny Enright and Willie to be oarsmen.

Once he had collected all the equipment he needed, we all walked to Merchant's Quay, lifted the currach from its cradle, loaded it, and then climbed in ourselves. I took my favourite place in the bow, while Uncle Andrew sat in the stern. Johnny and Willie took to the oars and we were off. Well, almost, as Johnny and Willie were not the best oarsmen you have ever seen. Our zigzagging passage was caused by their inability to work together, to the quiet frustration of Uncle Andrew. While the boys cursed each other in colourful language, Uncle Andrew was being hit by a lot of water as both would occasionally not dig in the oar deep enough resulting in water being flicked all over him. He bore it all with his slight smile, occasionally saying, "Will you not dig your oar a little deeper, Johnny."

"Aye, aye, sir," Johnny would reply with a wink at Willie.

Once clear of the heads, Uncle Andrew assessed the wind and tide and decided that we would fish off the island of Scattery. While the boys pulled generally in that direction, Uncle Andrew put out two trawling lines, and managed to catch eight reasonable sized mackerel, which he threw into the bottom of the boat. Johnny started singing. Johnny loved to sing, but he had a terrible voice. "Will you not stop that fokkin row," shouted Gerard. "Sure and you'll frighten all the fish away."

We eventually got to the end of the island and pulled into the lee side out of the current. We were just floating along gently. Uncle Andrew then opened a large can that he had brought. It contained liver, kidneys and intestines. He removed these from the tin and put it all into a muslin bag, which was then tied closed with a rope.

Next, he cut up some of the fish into large chunks. Finally, he carefully coiled the harpoon line. Attached to the end of this was 3 feet of wire trace and a hook that was the size of a man's fist. Once all the preparations had been done, he ordered the boys to pull out into the now fast-moving current. Once the current caught us, Uncle Andrew ordered the boys to ship their oars and we could all sit back and watch an expert at work.

First he hung the muslin bag with its contents over the side. We kept drifting for about twenty minutes. Occasionally, he would scatter some of the blood left in the bottom of the can. In our wake, we could see the trail we were leaving.

Suddenly, after he had been studying the sea around us, he turned. "Willie," he said. "Take her out further."

Willie responded immediately and taking both oars rowed us towards the middle of the Shannon between Scattery Island and Scough Point. As we moved, Uncle Andrew was busy putting more blood in the water and shaking the muslin bag.

Then Uncle Andrew did something that stunned us all, except Gerard, who had seen it all before of course. From his bag he removed a tambourine. Leaning over the side of the boat, he lowered the tambourine into the water and began shaking it violently. While he was doing this, he quietly explained the reason.

"The reason we have the offal and the blood, is that sharks can smell blood in the water for miles around. We have been setting a trail of blood. Now if a fish has been harpooned or attacked and is bleeding, it will also give off vibrations in the water. The sharks will attack easy prey, and nothing is easier than an injured fish. The tambourine is giving off the same vibrations as would an injured fish, so if there are any sharks around, they will come, wait and see."

He went on to explain that he had learned about this during his navy days. His ship had stopped at some islands in the South Pacific and he had been taught this method by a native of the islands. The native didn't use a tambourine, of course, but seashells wired together. It was Uncle Andrew's idea to substitute the shells with a tambourine.

After about ten minutes Gerard let out a shout. A shark's fin had appeared above the water about one hundred yards away.

"Okay, boys," said Uncle Andrew. "Now let's move gently." He took a whole mackerel and heaved it into the sea. The shark took it, but it was now only fifty yards away and another two had appeared. Uncle Andrew tossed pieces of fish, and we watched these huge six to seven feet fish thrashing after them.

Uncle Andrew picked up the hook and threaded a large piece of mackerel onto it, then with a couple of spins of the bait over his head, let it go. It hit the water with a splash, and we could see a shark move quickly to it. Uncle Andrew told both Willie and Johnny to get back on the oars and be ready.

The line ran out and then stopped. The rope was taut. "He swallowed that well enough," observed Uncle Andrew, and now the fight began. While this aging man battled a seven-foot shark, he kept up a running commentary instructing the boys on the direction he wanted them to row. He needed them to go against the current in order to tire the shark. Slowly, he reeled the shark closer and closer to the boat. It took about twenty minutes to get the shark to the boat, by which time both Johnny and Willie were breathing hard. I must admit that I was a little scared, as the shark looked so huge and I knew it could kill. Fortunately, there was not a plan to bring the shark into the boat. As soon as it was hard against the side of the currach, Uncle Andrew put it out of its misery with an axe blow into the head. It was then lashed to the boat for the journey back, or so we thought.

We noticed that the other sharks had not gone away— far from it. They seemed to be taking a great interest in us. Johnny was obviously frightened as he had never ever seen a shark, let alone be as close to them as he was then.

The next thing we knew was that this huge shark darted towards us opened its massive jaws and bit down on the dead shark attached to our boat. He vigorously shook his head, shaking our boat, as he tore a lump of flesh from the dead shark's side.

Gerard and me were shouting to Uncle Andrew as to

where we thought the next attack would come from. The next minute one came right under the bow, where I was sat, and hit the body hard, tearing another chunk from it while badly rocking the boat. At this point, Uncle Andrew, with a sad smile on his face, took the axe and cut our catch free.

"Ah well," sighed Uncle Andrew. "That will be that for today. Sometimes you get them home, and sometimes you don't." He turned to look at a very pale-faced Johnny. "Are you alright there, Johnny?" he asked. It would take a crowbar to get Johnny to go shark fishing again. Slowly, we zigzagged our way home. Even after all that time, there was no way that Johnny and Willie could get their timing right.

The earliest known photo of Joe Riley *(left)*, taken in 1947 at age 5; Katie Deloughery (center), and a young Lourda Shalloe *(right)*. Photo was taken at the back of No. 3 Pound St.

"Auntie May" Deloughery—at the very spot where Joe Riley first met his Auntie May. Joe had been waiting for Sean to make a kite at the gate of No. 3 Pound St.

"Uncle Andrew" Deloughery, Senior, taken around 1911 when
he first joined the British Navy. He was on the battle cruiser
Invincible at the Battle of Jutland during World War I.

The last known photo of Joe Riley *(standing)* taken in Kilrush in 1958 at the customs house quay about to head out sailing. Joseph Enright is in the foreground.

An aerial view looking southwest at Kilrush and the sea.
Francis Street in the center; Pound Street at the upper right.

The Deloughery's home at No. 3 Pound St., is third from right.
No. 1 has a boat outside it, showing that connections with the
sea remain strong.

The round tower and cathedral on Scattery Island just offshore Kilrush in the Shannon River. The tower is said to be more than 1,100 years old.

Joe Riley today, Manila, Philippines.

The last meeting of the surviving Deloughery family— *(l to r)* Willie and Andrew Deloughery, now deceased, Lulu and Joe.

CHAPTER SEVENTEEN

A Tragic Family Death

It was during my ninth year that I learned the meaning of grief. It is said that truth can be sometimes stranger than fiction. One night myself, Uncle Andrew and Senan Corbett were sat at the kitchen table playing cards. It was not with ordinary cards we were playing, but cards with letters of the alphabet on them. The purpose of the game was to spell words. It was the final game of the evening, and Uncle Andrew won handsomely by laying down the word "heaven." It could have been a message from God himself, as that night, Dr. Dick had to be called, and by the morning, Uncle Andrew, my mentor and friend, had passed away. Even though it was a blessing that his passing had been quick and painless, a cloud of deep sadness fell over the whole house.

He was laid out in his bed by Cissie Roughan, the midwife. Cissie was the one who helped people both into this world and out. Her favourite saying was, "There are more fathers than husbands in this town."

As was custom in Kilrush, the following evening the coffin was removed from the house and taken to be placed in front of the alter of St. Senan's Church. Everybody who passed away in Kilrush spent his or her last night before burial in the candlelit church. Gerard, Willie and Sean stayed all night with Uncle Andrew, praying that he be granted entrance into heaven.

The following morning, along with many friends and neighbours, we mournfully followed the Mass given by Father Ryan and assisted by Fathers Flynn and Coneady.

In the very front row sat Paddy Griffin and Paddy Brasil, Uncle Andrew's friends and shipmates, with tears unashamedly flowing down their faces.

At the end of the Mass, Gerard, Sean, Willie and Andrew, who had arrived from Germany only that morning, assisted by Johnny Enright and Joe O'Donnell lifted the coffin, placed it on their shoulders and carried Uncle Andrew out of the church to the waiting hearse.

The hearse moved off and we all fell in behind to follow it. Slowly, the hearse moved away towards the Convent, where it turned right and continued up the road to the crossroads where Reidy's Garage was located. We turned right into Henry Street and came into the square, proceeded past the Town Hall, the Manchester Martyrs monument then on down Frances Street. As we passed the shops, they would close their doors in respect. People on the footpath would stop and face the procession. The men would take off their caps, bow their heads and make the sign of the cross. The women would take out their Rosary beads and bless themselves. We walked down to the bottom of Frances Street, past the flourmill that my father built, past the railway station and up to the crossroads to Pella Road and Pound Street. We then turned left and walked all the way to Shanakyle Cemetery.

Uncle Andrew's last resting-place is the cemetery that later was so lovingly restored by Willie and some friends. Old and New Shanakyle were the main cemeteries for Kilrush. Shanakyle was host to at least two funerals a week. Funerals in Ireland were like a social outing, it was a chance to get away from the monotony of daily life and on occasions, to celebrate life and thank God for being alive.

Once Uncle Andrew had been gently and lovingly lowered into the family grave, the mourners turned to walk back to the house for the wake.

The wake was usually held in the home of the deceased and people would drink to their eternal life in the hereafter. It was a great excuse to drink however excessive it sometimes might turn out to be.

The wake was as much a part of the burial ceremony as was the Mass in the church. Virtually everyone left an amount of money, however little it was, to entertain their friends and neighbours on the day of their funeral. Death was as natural as anything else in our time. It seemed to be just one of those states where you pass from one thing into another.

All of Uncle Andrew's great friends were at his wake. Paddy Haugh and his family from Kilkee, Paddy Griffin who for the first time that I can ever remember had nothing to say, the pain he felt could be seen in his face. He sat behind the door with a bottle of stout and said nothing. Paddy Brasil, with a tear in his eye sat beside him and both of them stared at the floor in silence. In spite of my being young, I could plainly see that the pain and the loss was too much for both of them. Shipmates all their lives, they were like the three musketeers. They'd played, lived and went to war together. All three of them were at the battle of Jutland, one of the greatest battles of the First World War, and now they were two.

So many people came to the house that day with the customary knock on the opened door using the normal salutation "God bless all in this house."

This was the first occasion that I had experienced sorrow and grief.

It took quite a while for the house to get back to some normality. For weeks afterwards Auntie May would sit in the corner on her favourite chair by the fireside, quietly weeping. I would put my arm around her and I would cry along with her. I really missed my best friend and mentor. It was hard to come to terms with the fact that we would never fish together again.

CHAPTER EIGHTTEEN

My Mother Comes To Call

I suppose everybody has a bad year at some time in his or her life. Mine was definitely the twelve months that included my Uncle Andrew being taken from us. My family softened the grief I felt. My family? I was brought suddenly to earth by the announcement of my Auntie May that my mother was coming to visit me. She obviously believed I would be happy with this news. My mother?

What she didn't understand was that as my father had removed me from her when I was not even four years of age, I did not have a clue as to what she looked like, and neither did I have any feelings, except for fear. For many nights prior to her arrival I couldn't sleep. Stupid as it may seem, but I had grown to nearly nine years of age without having a mother. "Auntie" rolled off my tongue with ease, but how would I address my own mother? Did I call her mum, mummy, mama? I really did not have a clue.

Along with Sean, I had seen many pictures at Mars Cinema. One I remembered was a movie called "Mandy" starring Haley Mills. She had played a deaf and dumb girl, and the very first word she managed to say was "mummy." I decided that this would be the word to use. For days, I would practice saying it. "Mummy." I would say it when no one was around to hear. Even to my ear, it didn't sound the same as when Haley Mills had said it, but then, she didn't have a Clare accent.

The day of her expected arrival came. She would be travelling overnight on the Liverpool-Dublin ferry, and then would take the train to Limerick, arriving there at 1:30 in the afternoon. Auntie May had commissioned Gerald Griffin who regularly was contracted to drive people to and from Limerick. Gerald was given a photograph of my mother and told that she would have a small child with her, whom it turned out, was Olive, my yet unseen sister. Gerald had done this type of collection many times before for the people of Kilrush. He was as well known around Limerick railway station as he was around the town of Kilrush. Gerald had a fantastic memory. Many years later, on a visit back, I arrived in Limerick unannounced and on the off chance; I asked the ticket collector, "Have you seen the Kilrush driver, Gerald Griffin?"

"Sure and isn't he having a cup o' tay in the café over there," came the reply. I wandered over and entered the café, and sure enough, Gerald was sitting there. I walked up to his table and said, "Hello Gerald. And how the devil are you?"

Gerald looked up and a huge smile broke his face as he extended his hand to shake mine.

"Would you have a spare seat back to Kilrush, Gerald?" I asked.

"I'll always find space for you, Riley," he answered, as I sat down. Then his first question was. "How's your mother?" Then the questions flowed thick and fast until he knew everything that had happened to me. It was the same with everybody. On the journey back, Gerald would bring you up to date on all the happenings in Kilrush. He was like a Willie, but on wheels. Gerald was Paddy Griffin's nephew so he knew how to make his stories interesting.

After dinner, I stayed in the house with Auntie May. I was both excited and scared. Time seemed to pass so slowly, but eventually, at about 3:30 in the afternoon, we heard Gerald blow his horn. Auntie May and me went to the door. I had my arm around Auntie May as I was so nervous. My mother got out of the car and started to walk toward us up the path. I could see that tears were streaming down her face. She reached us and put her arms around me, hugging me tightly to her, crying all the time and not saying a word. I still held on to the skirt of Auntie May, my security in this world. Gerald had followed her with her suitcase and stood behind her. The scene must have been very emotional because even Auntie May was dabbing at her eyes.

"Gerald," said Auntie May. "Put the bags in the kitchen will you?"

"Yes, ma'am," answered Gerald pushing past us.

"Would you like a cup of tay?" asked Auntie May.

"No thank you, ma'am," answered Gerald. "I still have to go to Kilkee."

As he came back out, my mother let go of me, opened her purse and paid Gerald the one-pound fee.

While all of this was going on, I glanced at my sister, Olive, who stood there holding onto my mothers skirt. She was about 3 years of age, had very blond near white hair tied with blue ribbons. She had on a white dress that flared out and a waistband that matched the colour of her ribbons. Her skin was very fair, nearly white, unlike the people of Kilrush with our weather beaten complex.

The wind that was whipped up of the Atlantic Ocean gave us all a red face and slight tanned complex. Paddy Griffin used to say that a lot of people who came to the town thought we had a good tan. Then he would explain in his real Irish lilt, "Will you go away our dat. Sure it's not a tan at all. This is rust from all the rain we get."

When the greetings were over, we all went along the passage to the kitchen. I had my first opportunity to have a real good look at my mother.

The first thing I noticed was her hair. My mother had long dark, wavy hair. It reminded me of some of the film stars. She also had a very good figure and was a woman who could make heads turn. She was about 5 feet 6 inches tall and dressed well. In reality, my mother was a beautiful looking woman.

"Would you like a cup of tay?" asked Auntie May, as soon as we were in the kitchen.

"I would love one," answered my mother. It was the first time I had heard her talk, and she talked so differently from all of us. My mother kept pulling me to her and hugging and kissing me. I was more used to the Auntie May style of just pecking the top of my head and her "Away with you." I decided to break off the engagement, so I said to Auntie May, "I am just going to Senan's house." Auntie May understood. She understood everything. She just nodded, and I escaped with my thoughts in turmoil.

Senan only lived across the road from us, and we were the best of friends. Having been granted permission, I was out the door and down the path so fast it was not funny. I ran across the road and into Senan's house. His mother was making griddlecake for tea. The griddlecake had a beautiful aroma that meandered through the whole house clearly announcing what was cooking for tea. In spite of the trauma, I was excited about my mother arriving. I told Senan that both my mother and sister were sitting at that moment in our kitchen at home. "Senan," I said. "You've got to come over and meet my mother, you too Mrs. Corbett. I have a mother and a sister."

It sounded strange to my own ears......a mother. For as long as I could remember, people around the town had asked me about my mother and father, and I had no answer. Now I was the same as other boys—I had a mother.

Senan and I ran from the house, out of the door, across the road and up the path. We were out of breath by the time we reached the front door. Walking up the hall to the kitchen, I had to keep tugging at the sleeve of Senan, urging him to have a look at my mother who we could hear talking to Auntie May.

As we entered the kitchen, I could see that Auntie May had given my mother the seat of honour, the chair in the corner next to the range, her own chair.

"Mummy," I said, for the first time. "This is my friend Senan." I didn't feel very comfortable with the word "mummy."

Senan stood there open mouthed. In Kilrush at that time, people who came from a foreign country were put on a pedestal. After all, if you came from a foreign country you probably had money and good breeding the same as in the movies. You never saw movies that had people like those in Kilrush in them.

My mother smiled and beckoned Senan to her. She touched his face. "Hello, Senan," she said. "How are you?"

Senan appeared petrified. "I'm fine thanks, ma'am," he answered.

Suddenly, my mother sat upright. "Oh," she said. "I nearly forgot. I have some presents for you."

She stood up and went to her bag. She removed a number of packages wrapped in brown paper and tied with string. One package she handed to me she said, "This is a special present, Joe. It's from your Nana."

I didn't have a clue what or who a Nana was, but I opened it just the same. It was only later, on one of our walks together, that she explained it was her mother. In fact, in many later talks she appeared confused at my lack of knowledge of my real family.

The package contained a red fire engine with lights. The other packages contained various toys from uncles and aunts of whom I had never heard.

She then reached in her bag and drew out one more package. "Senan," she said. "This is for you."

Senan's face lit up, a present and from overseas. I was happy that my mother had not forgotten my friend Senan. When he opened it, we saw it contained an airplane kit of balsa wood, that once put together, could be flown.

Just then, with a tap on the door and a "God bless all in this house," Senan's mother, Mrs. Corbett came in, closely followed by Katie and Lulu. Because of the arrival of my mother, they had left their work early, Katie from the dressmaker's and Lulu from her cook's job at the Monastery. Katie was very shy, although before my mother left, they were to become very close. Lulu on the other hand, together with Mrs. Corbett, kept praising my mother, embarrassing her by telling her that she looked and dressed like a "fillum" star. Soon though, Lulu was asking her about the latest fashions and music in England. I kept trying to show my mother my fishing rod, made for me by Uncle Andrew.

Next in was Mary, home from her job as cook and housekeeper to Mrs. Glynn, who lived next door to the Monastery. The kettle was kept hot and the little enamel teapot, also sitting of the range top, was continually replenished. With all of these women in the kitchen, it was a relief when Willie arrived. Being a bank messenger, it was easy for him to drop in at any time. He took over the conversation.

"Hallo, Mrs. Riley. How is Joe?" he asked, referring to my father.

"He's fine, thank you," replied my mother. "He's working in Brazil. Please call me Doris."

Well, that was something. I now knew my mother's name.

"Well Doris," continued Willie. "How are the rest of the family?" before she could answer, he added, "Geeze. You sure have a way to wear clothes." My mother blushed. Before too long, however, Willie had extracted a great deal of information from her that would surely be relayed around the town on the morrow. Willie was the equivalent of a television chat show host.

While all of this excitement was going on, my sister Olive was sleeping in the front parlour. This was a very small room, about 12 feet by square, with a window that looked out over the front garden. Down the lane one could see Glynn's flourmill in the background, where my father used to work.

I was allowed to take time off school while my mother visited and everyday we would go for a walk up to the town and look at the shops, not that there were really any interesting shops in Kilrush. However one shop took her fancy in Moore Street and that was Lynch's shop. This shop sold the local souvenirs of Kilrush and my mother purchased quite a few, many of which she kept until the day she died. Her favourite souvenir was a green mug with Kilrush written across it. Altogether she purchased four of them so you can understand why Joe Lynch was very glad to see us each day. Joe was the owner of the shop. He was a small tubby man with a big round face and his hair was always kept in place with Brylcreem. When we finished at Joe's shop we would walk from Moore Street back up to the square and go to May Dwyer's shop.

May Dwyer was a lovely lady with short black hair and half-moon glasses, a tiny petite woman who always seemed to be in a hurry. When you walked in the shop, May would be behind the counter. She would bow her head slightly and look at you over her glasses. May and her sister both manned the shop. Her sister was totally different to May, having long blonde hair. Neither had ever married and they lived together over the shop.

On Thursdays, Sean and myself would also wait at May Dwyer's shop for the arrival of the bus from Limerick as it carried our precious copies of Beano and Dandy comics. The Limerick Kilkee bus would cross the square and drive down Frances Street to the railway station near the flourmill. It would drop off parcels at the station then would come back to the Square and park outside of Mrs. Crotty's pub and May Dwyer's shop. We waited impatiently for May to unpack her parcel and then got our comics.

My mother liked May Dwyer's shop as it stocked all Irish lace and linen as well as a lot of toys, religious books and pictures.

Later, we would walk across the square, past the library, around the corner and into Frances Street. As soon as we were around this corner we could see The Creek and the mouth of the River Shannon.

As the week went by it became very obvious to my mother that I was totally ignorant of my real family back in England and this I believe disturbed her more and more as the time passed. The more she spoke to me the more she realized that I had no idea at all about the life of my family in England. She would talk to me about my Nana, Aunt Elsie, my brothers and sisters. She showed me photos of them but I never knew who they were. Auntie May became restless and not very happy as my mother's stay progressed. I had no idea why, but it became evident on the Sunday afternoon. Auntie May took me aside and asked me if I would like to go to England with my mother for a holiday. Although for me the idea was very exciting, the pain in Auntie May's face was evident as she spoke to me. Auntie May was adamant that I had to come back home to Kilrush and that I was only going for a two weeks holiday to meet my family.

Willie, Gerard and Sean had a talk with me before I left for England and they gave me some money to spend.

CHAPTER NINETEEN

Land Of My Birth

We left on a Tuesday morning. Gerald Griffin picked us up in the car from home. Auntie May was crying, she was obviously very upset as she hugged me and kissed me.

My mother assured her, "Auntie May. I promise he will be back in two weeks." Auntie May could not speak and she was so upset her hanky was all wet with tears.

We got the usual blessing and holy water thrown all over us to make sure our journey would be safe.

Gerard looked so sad as did Willie and Sean. Lulu, Katie and Mary were crying and kissed me before I walked out the door.

I suppose it was the fear that my mother would keep me and not let me return to Kilrush.

It was 7:30 in the morning when Gerald arrived because we had to catch the 10 a.m. train from Limerick to Dublin. I sat in the front seat next to Gerald and my mother sat in the back with my sister on her knee. It took about an hour and a half to get to Limerick over the bumpy roads. Not very much of the road between Kilrush and Ennis was paved. The road was also very narrow, so that the numerous carts, pulled by horse or donkey, moving milk from the farms to the creamery, also slowed our progress. Once we had passed through the narrow streets of Ennis, the road improved considerably, and we made better speed. Our journey took us past the ruined castles of Clare and Bunratty, until finally we crossed the bridge into Limerick and entered the rail station.

Limerick station was huge, a far cry from our station in Kilrush. The station was totally roofed over.

Gerald helped us into the station with our bags, my mother had Olive in her arms and I carried my own little brown case.

We walked up the steps and into the station. My mother bought a ticket for me and we went into the station tearoom. I had a bottle of orange juice and my mother had a cup of tea. Our train was standing at the station. There was some time before it was due to depart, so we put our bags into a compartment, and then walked along the platform to look at the engine. Compared to our local West Clare train, this one was huge.

We walked back and boarded the train. Soon it started the long haul to Dublin, stopping at every station along the way. Eventually we arrived in Dublin at 3.30 in the after-noon. We caught the bus to North Shore Docks for the boat. The ship was called the "MV Munster". We were early and the place was closed when we got there, so we waited outside until it opened at 6 p.m. The boat train, as it was called, did not leave for Liverpool until 8 p.m. We were the first on board the boat and mother found a quiet place where we sat down on a wooden bench-type seat. I wanted to have a look around the ship but mother would not let me stray far.

We left Dublin on time. I was by then getting tired of all the travel. We were in second class at the stern of the boat. I fell asleep on the wooden bench close to my mother. I was on one side of her and Olive slept on the other. We awoke early in the morning just as dawn was breaking. The ship had pulled into Birkenhead to off-load some cattle. I could see the cattle running down the ramp into cattle yards below.

We then set off across the Mersey River to the Pier where we got off the ship, walked down the gangplank and into a big warehouse. The customs men were standing behind some tables and they waved us by. We got on a bus to Lime Street Station to catch a train to Darlington in the North of Yorkshire. "Can we have something to eat?" I asked my mother.

"I'll just get your ticket and find out the time of the train, and then we will eat," answered my mother.

After mother had bought me my breakfast, we boarded the train to Newcastle, changed at Darlington to catch a train to Thornaby-on-Tees.

At Darlington station, on the platform was an old steam train. It was the first steam train in the history of the British Railways, The Locomotion.

We reached Thornaby after about 30 minutes. My sister May and brothers Keith and David were waiting outside the gate of the station. Olive was all excited and ran to David.

At my first glimpse of my newfound family, my stomach turned over. I couldn't believe what I saw. Throughout her stay with us in Ireland, my mother received many comments about her appearance and dress sense. It was puzzling therefore as to why her children looked like a bunch of ratbags. The clothes they wore were ragged and torn. David had on short pants, a shirt that was dirty and a pullover with holes in the sleeves. On his feet he had an old brown pair of sandals and no socks. They all looked as though they had not washed for a week. David and Keith had a tidemark around their neck. The sleeve of Keith's shirt was marked from wiping his nose. None of them had combed their hair.

By way of contrast, my clothes were all hand-made by Katie. I had a jacket made-to-measure as were my short pants. I had new black, lace up shoes and knee length socks.

As we all met together, I made my first mistake. "Mummy," I started as a beginning to a question. David looked at Keith. "Oh, mummy," he said, and they, along with

May, collapsed laughing. They all spoke with a thick Geordie accent so that I could not understand them. My Irish accent was equally indecipherable to them. I soon discovered that 'mummy" was not a word in their vocabulary.

My brothers and sister had no idea how I felt and they had no idea what they had done in those first few seconds. They made me feel so bad and to them it was nothing I'm sure. They had no idea of the pain and hurt they had just caused me. I was now made to feel different and I was different. They looked me over and then my clothes and David said I was a toffee boy. Whatever that was I had no idea but I knew it was not an endearing remark.

The three of them clustered around mother asking if she had brought them any presents. Then David and Keith picked up the suitcases and we made our way up a ramp to the street. I kept totally silent, almost as if in shock.

We waited at the bus stop until a bus came along, which we boarded. I had never seen a double-decker bus before let alone rode on one. We stayed down stairs and as my mother knew the conductress, she did not charge us any fare. We got off at the end of Beechwood Road and Keith ran on ahead.

We lived at 31 Beechwood Road, on the corner of Popular Road. The first thing I noticed was that the garden was the worst in the street. It was a mess. It had been allowed to just run wild.

We walked in the back door and entered the house. This was even worse. It was more than a mess. Keith told his mother that they had all chipped in to clean the house. I just thought that if this was what is was like after it had been tidied up, what must it have been like before?

The house was a three-bedroom terrace with this house at the end of the block. It had a living room downstairs, a small kitchen, and as you came in the backdoor, on the right was a coalhouse and the left was the toilet.

I soon learned to forget calling my mother "mummy."

My siblings either used the "mam", or if they needed something from her, they would then call her "mother".

Very shortly after we arrived my Nana came together with Auntie Elsie. I liked my Nana. She looked tall to me with very white hair wrapped up in a scarf that was tied around her head. Nana asked me a lot of questions, and both she and Auntie Elsie seemed amused at my Irish accent. I was beginning to feel like an exhibit at the zoo.

My youngest brother, who hadn't been at the station to meet us, came in and asked, "Who is that?"

"Kenny," answered my mother. "This is your brother, Joe."

Ken said nothing and just looked at me.

Auntie Elsie took me to her house across the road in Elm Grove. The house was beautiful compared to my mother's as at least all the furniture was nice and clean. Auntie Elsie I think took pity on me and she spent a lot of time with me.

My biggest shock was to come. Keith took me upstairs to show me where I would sleep. There were two beds in the room, a double bed and a single bed. I was to sleep in the single bed. The beds had no sheets on them. The double bed had a blanket and an old army overcoat on it; it was soiled from bedwetting. The smell of the room was unbearable. It was filthy and I had to sleep there. My mother could see the shock on my face and asked if I was all right. I just nodded. I had a blanket and an army overcoat on my bed. This is not what I was used to. We may have been poor in Kilrush but everything was clean. That night I went to bed and opened the window for some fresh air. David, Keith and Kenny complained because it was cold. When they went to sleep I went downstairs and slept on the sofa. By now my mother knew that I was not happy.

I joined in a game of football in the street. As the ball came to me I caught it in my hands and blasted the ball past the dumbfounded goalkeeper. Everyone stood in amazement and looked at me.

"What the fuck was that?" said David. "You can't do that."

"Do what?" I replied.

"You can't pick up the ball, that's what," answered a now angry David.

"Why not?" I asked.

"Because this is fucking football and you don't pick up the fucking ball," shouted David in exasperation. Jimmy Roberts was laughing, but I had spoilt the game and it was not funny to them.

In Kilrush we swear a lot. With some people every other word is 'fuck' but its not said in the same way, it sounds more like 'fok' and it does not have the same connotation that it has when they say it in England. Swearing is part of every day life in Kilrush and an accepted part of the language, well at our end of town it was. Swearing was innocent and inoffensive, unlike in England where it was crude and hurtful and they meant it when they said it.

Auntie May swore like a trooper at times, as did everyone in the house. Especially on a Sunday morning prior to going to mass when everyone was getting dressed up.

"Sean. Have you got my new fokking shirt on?" asked Willie.

"Have I fok. This is my shirt," answers Sean.

"Will you fokkers stop it and get ready. You'll be late for Mass," interposed Gerard. "Riley. Are you fokking ready yet?"

"No," I would reply. "I'm fokking not and anyway I'm not going as I'm a Protestant." I was always a protestant when it suited the occasion

"Boyyo, I'll kick your fokkin' arse all the way to the church if you're not ready in a minute." This was normal Sunday morning but no one took offence at it. This was part of the culture of the West Coast and its language.

I was now ridiculed more than ever before and I was thrown out of the soccer side in the street. I had never heard of soccer. I played for the school and I was good as a gaelic footballer, the only football I knew, and yes we did pick the ball up. I walked back into the house visibly upset and mother knew that I was not happy. Picking the ball up was a topic at teatime and I was again that stupid Irish clown who picked up the ball in a game of football.

On Saturday, Auntie Elsie took me to Stockton market. The market was in the middle of the High Street and I remember all the stalls, people shouting out and all the things I had never seen before. I spent ages at the pet stall. I had never seen a budgie or a gold fish so it was extraordinary to see all of these things. No one in Kilrush ever heard of a budgie or a gold fish, they just did not exist. Auntie Elsie wanted to buy me a budgie but I declined, thanking her. I think she liked my gentle way and my manners.

In Kilrush I may have been considered to be a rascal but a harmless rascal. My brothers though were just wild. They had no manners, had no idea how to behave with people, at home or anywhere else for that matter.

While they were at school I was left at home with my mother. She would take me to different places to meet relatives I had never even heard of, such as Uncle Jimmy and Aunt Polly. Aunt Polly, Aunt Elsie and my mother all worked on the buses as conductors otherwise known as clippies.

On Sunday, May and David took me to Stockton to meet Granddad and Grandma Riley. My grandmother was very tubby lady with short curly hair and she wore glasses. She spoke with a real Geordie accent, as did my grandfather. I enjoyed the company of my grandfather. He spoke in a gentle manner. He wore a hat with a black rim band, a shirt with no collar and a waistcoat. He smoked a pipe and seemed to have matches in every pocket. He took me out to see his pride and joy, "his roses." He grew these in both the front and back gardens and the place was so neat and tidy. He was so proud of his roses and his vegetable patch.

When we came back into the house, Uncle Bill and Auntie Winnie were there. I immediately liked them. For once, I was not the only one with a funny accent. Uncle Bill came from Northern Ireland and he had a soft strong Northern Irish accent that just rolled off his tongue.

"Where do you live, Joe?" he asked.

"In Kilrush, Co Clare," I answered.

"I was in Limerick once. Is that anywhere near you?" he asked.

"Yes. We are about 60 miles away by road," I said.

"I see. Do you go to school there?" he asked.

"I do indeed. At the Christian Brothers School," I said.

We conversed for a while. David was creating havoc as usual.

Auntie Winnie sat on the sofa. She had a great sense of humour and we laughed about all sorts. I think most of the laughter was at my accent because they could not understand me. Uncle Bill could understand me however and they were laughing with me not at me. At my mother's house everyone laughed at me.

This was a welcome break and I did not want to go back to Beechwood Road at the end of the afternoon.

I became increasingly restless. My brothers and their friends called me various names, none of them complimentary. You Irish bastard, you fucking Mick, and so on. My mother sensed that I wanted to get back to Kilrush.

"Mother," I said. "Can I go home?"

"Yes Joe," answered mother, sadly. "But we can't get hold of them in Kilrush. You are not due back there until Wednesday week."

This was on a Monday. I really didn't think I could stand over another week of this.

"I can get hold of them." I told her.

"How, Joe?" she asked

"We have a 'phone in the Square." I told her. "I can call the town."

"What do you mean?" asked my mother.

"People from all over the world 'phone the town, even from America and Australia," I explained.

Obviously my mother was intrigued. "You show me how to do it," she instructed.

I picked up the 'phone. It was about 6 p.m. when I asked the operator to put me through to the exchange in Kilrush, Ireland. A few moments later I hear a voice with an Irish accent announce it was Dublin exchange. Our operator then asked for Kilrush and I heard a familiar voice.

"Hello, Mary," I said. "Is that you?"

"Yes, it is," she replied. "Who's calling?"

"It's me," I said. "Joe Riley calling from England."

"Joe Riley is it?" she said. "I'd heard you had gone over there. How are you? Fetin it's a grand life you have, Riley. Trottin' all over the world."

"I'm fine, Mary," I replied. "Could you put me through to the Square?"

Mary was not just a telephone operator, but also worked at the post office. She lived down our lane and knew everyone that lived overseas. Mary gave a new meaning to the word service. If no one answered at the Square, Mary would make sure that the message got through to your family one way or another.

Kilrush had about twenty telephones in total. One of them was a 'phone box in the middle of the town, in the Square close to Mrs. Considines shop near the statue of the Maid of Erin.

No matter where you were in the world, you could get hold of your family by calling this phone box in the middle of the town. Someone walking by would answer.

"Hello," a voice said.

"Hello there," I said. "This is Joe Riley in England."

"Fokking hell Riley, how are you?" said the voice.

"Who's that?" I asked.

"John Doyle," answered the voice.

"Fokkin hell, Doyle, how's things?" I asked.

"Geeze. Brother Gleeson is giving us all a cat of a time at the moment," he informed me.

"I'm fokkin glad I'm over here," I exclaimed. "What's he doing?"

"He's got the fokkin singing rage again and wants a choir," said John. "We couldn't sing in a hundred fokkin years."

"John," I said. "Can you go down and tell Willie that I will ring back in an hour?"

"I'll go down now," answered John.

John Doyle went to school with me. His father had a bar next to Keating's butcher's shop, which in turn was next door to Tom Joe Reidy's garage at the top of Henry Street.

My mother was astonished that I could call a town in the middle of nowhere in another country and get someone just like that. Sure enough, one-hour later we went through the same procedure.

"Hello Joe," said Mary. "Willie is above in the Square waiting for your call. I'll put you through."

The phone only rang once and Willie picked it up. "Riley. How are you?" he asked.

"I'm grand," I replied. "And how's everyone there?"

I think Willie was half expecting bad news from me and was anticipating I was going to tell him that I would not be returning to Kilrush. I could almost hear his sigh of relief when I told him I wanted to go home. I then handed the telephone to my mother and left them in conversation while I went outside. In a few minutes she came out and told me that I would be returning home on Thursday. I was overjoyed.

She looked a little sad as she walked back into the house

but I just wanted to get back to Kilrush as soon as I could. I was very unhappy with all the ridicule and the fighting that went on within her house. Real family or not, in my case blood was certainly not thicker than water. I may have been confused when I left Kilrush as to where I belonged, but there was no doubt in my mind now. I wanted to get back to my real family. It now seemed true. One could choose your friends, but not your relatives.

CHAPTER TWENTY

The Return Of The Prodigal

Thursday morning arrived and everyone was getting ready to go to school. I was ready to go to the station and start my journey back to Ireland. My mother had not explained anything to me until we were on the train to Darlington. It was then that she started to give me lots of instructions. We were on the platform of Thornaby station when the train pulled in. The platform shook, the noise was deafening and steam hissed from the engine. I was frightened and mother could sense it as she put her arm around me.

We got into a carriage and proceeded to Darlington. At Darlington we crossed the platform and passed The Locomotion then waited for the Liverpool boat train. We boarded the train and my mother started to give me the instructions once again. This was a situation of "have envelopes, will travel."

My mother had given me six envelopes, each of which was placed in a different pocket of my clothing.

"Now, Joe," said my mother. "Tell me which envelope is which?"

"The one in my inside pocket is for the porter at the station," I commenced. "The one in my right hand pocket is for the porter at the boat," I continued. "The one in my left pocket is for the bus driver."

I stopped and thought. "In my back pocket is the envelope for the steward on the boat, and in my top pocket is for the porter at Dublin Station." My mother beamed. "Well done, Joe," she said, with tears in her eyes.

She was visibly upset as we got closer to York Station because she had explained that she would get off at York and I was to continue on my own with my envelopes. I was not frightened at the prospect.

"Make sure you stay on the train until the end of the line and then see the porter," said mother.

"Yes Ma'am," I responded.

"And stay inside the boat. Do you understand?" she asked.

"Yes Ma'am," I said again.

In each envelope there was half a crown with a note. All the envelopes were sealed and I had to hand them over as instructed.

Mother got off the train at York and said goodbye; we only had a few minutes before it pulled out again. Mother was crying and kissed me.

The guard blew the whistle and waved his flag, mother walked beside the train.

"Joe," she shouted. "Be a good boy. I love you."

I waved goodbye and lost her in the steam and the smoke of the train. For the first time I felt broken hearted and torn apart. I sat back in my seat and just cried and cried. I was totally lost in a way and my world had drastically changed.

A lady and her husband were sat on the other side of the carriage and she noticed my distress. "Are you all right, son?" she asked. The tears were falling down my face and I said nothing. She put her arm around me and consoled me for a while.

We eventually arrived in Liverpool. As instructed I got my little brown case and made sure that I was in Liverpool.

I could read the sign but I still checked with another passenger.

"Is this Liverpool?" I asked.

"It sure is," was the reply. "Everyone gets off here; it's the end of the line."

I found a porter and gave him the envelope. It had porter written on his hat and he opened the envelope. Then he said, "Come with me, lad." He took me across the station and out of the side of the station and he spoke with the driver of the bus. "Drop this lad off at the boat will ya?" he asked.

"No problems," answered the driver. "I'll make sure he gets there." I sat in the front of the bus, close to the driver and off we went. We were at the boat in minutes.

"You get out here," instructed the driver. "Are you going to Dublin?"

"Yes," I said.

"Then go through those doors over there," he said, pointing in the direction I should go. My ticket was a combined ticket all the way to Dublin. I sat in the waiting room until it was time to board. They started boarding at 6 p.m. It was the same boat I had arrived on so I went to the same place where I had stayed with mother and Olive. There was a small café on board and very few people. I approached the steward and handed him an envelope. He looked at me strange at first, read the letter and put the money in his pocket.

"Sit over there," he said, pointing at some large chairs. I duly obeyed and went and sat down. "You like a cup of tay?" he asked. I nodded. "Where have you come from?" asked the steward. I told him and he asked where I was going.

"I am going home to Kilrush," I told him. "I have to get the Limerick train tomorrow morning from Dublin."

"I live close to the station," said the steward. "I'll take you there in the morning."

The ship was now moving and people were settling down for the night. The steward had a bit of work to do before he finished; he had to clean the toilets close by. He had a mop and a bucket to do the floors. I sat on the toilet seat until he finished. He was a real nice guy about 25 years old, looked very smart in his blue uniform and had a sense of humour. One customer came up to him and said. "Can I have a cup tea please?"

"Certainly sir," answered the steward. "That will be one shilling."

"How much?" cried the customer.

"One shilling, sir," he said with a smile

"That's outrageous," was the response.

"Look at it this way sir," answered the steward. "How much would it cost you to buy a boat to have a cup of tea on?"

The man grumbled and stormed off, the steward looked at me and winked.

I fell asleep and woke early in the morning, my friend the steward was back on duty and looking after me. He gave me a cup of tea and told me that it would only take a few minutes after we had docked for him to be able to take me to Euston Station to catch the train to Limerick.

We got off the boat and there was a bus waiting just outside the gate. We drove through the streets of Dublin following the river all the way past O'Connell Street, The Half Penny Bridge and on past the Guinness brewery.

I arrived at the station, expressed my thanks to the kindly ship's steward and I went to find a porter. Sure enough there was a porter. It was now 6:45 a.m. in the morning. I handed him the envelope; he opened it, put the money in his pocket and read the note. "Come with me young lad," he said. I followed him outside the station to the ticket office. "Do you have money on you?" he asked. I told him I had. "This young lad needs a ticket to Limerick," he told the ticket seller.

I paid the money, got given my ticket and he took me back into the station to the café. He had a word with the waiter and he said, "Sit over there" pointing at a table.

A waiter came over and asked, "Have you had breakfast?"

I said that I hadn't.

"Would you like some?" he asked.

"Yes please," I said "but how much is it?" I was now conscious of the money left that my mother gave me.

"Two and six pence," answered the waiter.

Thanks," I said. "I will have egg, bacon and some bread, please."

My train was not due to leave until 8 a.m. so I had time on my hands. In the meantime the porter popped in to see if I was okay.

"This train," he explained, "has two sections and I need to put you on the part that goes to Limerick. When it reaches Limerick Junction it splits into two. One part goes to Cork and we don't want you going there do we?" he said with a smile. "The other half will go to Limerick. Are you all right with that?"

I had a nice table and was looking forward to going home to Kilrush. I knew someone would be there waiting for me when I got off the train at Limerick. I was thinking that it maybe Gerard or Willie.

My breakfast arrived and it was really good to have real food. I was really enjoying it and I was on my last mouth full of lovely bacon when the waiter intervened as he filled my cup again. "Are you a Catholic?" he asked.

"Yes," I answered. "Why do you ask?"

"Well. Today is Friday and you have eaten meat," he said.

My God, I thought. What a terrible sin. I'm sure I'll go to hell for eating a bit of bacon.

He went on to explain that it was not a sin because I did not know that it was Friday. I had totally forgotten. I had one very good other reason, I was not a Catholic, but I was not going to tell him that.

The time came for boarding the train and the porter was there. "Let's go, young man," he said. I said thanks to the waiter and joined the porter.

It was a long boring journey and I eventually arrived at Limerick Station at 1:30 in the afternoon.

I had a surprise waiting when I arrived, as it was not Gerard or Willie waiting for me. My Auntie May was there at the end of the platform with Katie. I ran down the platform and into Auntie May's arms. She hugged me and kissed me and so did Katie. Gerald Griffin was on the sidelines watching all of this as he had done many times before with other reunions.

Auntie May was crying and drying her eyes, she was now looking for my mother. "Where is your mother?" she said. I told her I was on my own. Well, Auntie May went bananas. "Jesus, Mary and Joseph, have you come all that way on your own?" She asked. "Mother of God, the woman is mad. Jesus Christ she is crazy." She looked at Katie. "Did you hear what he said?" she asked.

"That's dreadful," said Katie. "Anything could have happened to him."

"I just can't believe this," continued Auntie May.

We walked out of the station to Gerald's car and headed back to Kilrush. I had to give a full explanation to her on the way. When we got home we had tea and she went through the whole affair again.

"I have never heard of anything so bizarre as to send a nine-year-old boy across the Irish Sea with envelopes," Willie said. "Someone is not right in the head."

My mother lost a lot of respect after this affair and was not mentioned again.

Auntie May went off the deep end again when she unpacked my case. Some of my clothes were missing and they had not been cleaned. Never-the-less, I was home. It was time for me to cross the road to visit Senan and Mrs. Corbett. As far as the journey was concerned, I was just glad to be back in Kilrush with the people I knew. At the time I really did not think that it was a great issue, but others in the house certainly did.

CHAPTER TWENTY ONE

My Kind Of People

I once counted the bars in Kilrush. There were thirty-five bars for a population of 2,800 people and that equated to one bar for every eighty people in town. Well you would never go dry in this town. The butcher's shop had on one side the meat and on the other side of the shop a bar. It was the same with the grocers. If you went into O'Shea's on Henry Street, on one side were all the vegetables and food and on the other side the bar.

The belief was that whenever an alcoholic died somewhere in the world he was reincarnated in the town of Kilrush for it was an alcoholic's dream, although we had our fair share of drunks as well. It was a hard life in the 1940s and 50s.

Some places were purely pubs. There was Paddy's Bar, McAuliffe's Bar, Doyle's Bar and of course the most famous of them all, Crotty's Bar. The fame of this bar was due to the landlady, Mrs. Elizabeth (Lizzie) Crotty, who became known throughout Ireland for her skill at playing traditional Irish tunes on her concertina.

Except to the locals of Kilrush, Mrs. Crotty was relatively unknown until the early 1950's. She could neither read nor write music in any of the conventional systems, but she could commit a tune to paper by giving each key a number, and using a symbol to denote a press or draw. Her style of playing was relatively unadorned, but it was very rhythmic, due to the fact that her music was played for dancers. Her two most popular tunes were "The Wind that Shakes the Barley" and "The Reel with the Beryl". These tunes brought out the very best in her style of playing on her Lachenal concertina. When my father had been in Kilrush in the late forties, he and Mrs. Crotty were wonderful friends as he was brilliant on the piano and they often accompanied each other when playing at local weddings or dances. She was a beautiful, unassuming woman who, in the long summer evenings, would often perch herself on a stool outside of the pub and play to us children.

During the mid 1950's her fame spread as a result of some recording sessions which Ciarán MacMathuna and the R.T.E., the Irish National Broadcasting Service, held in her house in the Square. He played her music frequently on his radio programs. In those years, Crotty's of the Square in Kilrush was visited regularly by musicians. One could be sure of a welcome, and a few tunes at almost any time of the day or night.

During her travels around the country she met and played with many musicians. In Dublin she met Mrs. Harrington who played the fiddle, and they became close friends. They were both members of the Pipers Club in Thomas Street, Dublin and they travelled to many of the Fleadhs together. Mrs. Crotty didn't take part in competitions but she enjoyed listening to the various musicians.

Even though she made no commercial recordings, she did make two private ones, a solo and a duet with Mrs. Harrington. Consequently there is very little of her music on record. However, when R.T.E. produced an L.P. to commemorate fifty years of Irish radio, they included one of Mrs. Crotty's items from the archives. The tune chosen was

"Geary's Reel", which Ciarán MacMathuna had recorded with her.

Although she passed away in 1969, she always has a warm place in my heart. I can hear her now, as she sat on her stool playing, saying to me, "How are you, Riley? Behavin' yourself, are ya?"

Who, living in Kilrush at that time, could ever forget John Joe O'Shea? John Joe was probably the most well know character in Kilrush. He was a gentle soul who spent most of his day in Mrs. O'Dea's shop on Henry Street. Everyone in the town knew John Joe. His claim to fame was something he did passionately and with genuine feelings. He marched by the side of every hearse in every Kilrush funeral, whether he was acquainted with the deceased or not. He marched alongside Uncle Andrew's hearse while we all trailed behind. If there was a parade of any kind, be it the Boy Scouts or whatever, John Joe marched alongside the baton major. Even when the Kilrush football team celebrated the winning of the Clare football final, against Miltown Malbay by parading around Kilrush, John Joe was there at the front, in his rightful place.

John Joe was only a little man, with a ferret-like face, but a more gentle person you would never wish to meet. The only time he showed any passion was when he was told that it was intended to grow trout in the town's reservoir at Knockerra. He was 'reliably' informed that the fingerlings would find their way into the distribution system and regularly emerge from the taps, ruining a good cup of tea. John Joe was so incensed he decided that he would run for election to the town council to put a stop to the plan. To be honest, nobody took John Joe that seriously. He would make speeches strongly criticizing the council's plan.

That year, Johnny Enright was also up for election. As the small number of voters were known, it was easy to calculate just how many votes were required to sure of victory.

It was the practice that once the candidate had obtained this number of votes, that he would give the excess to another candidate of his choice.

Johnny easily exceeded his target, and, being a kind man who didn't want to see John Joe embarrassed by having only a few votes, allocated his surplus to John Joe. Unknown to Johnny, virtually every other winning candidate had done the same. When the votes were counted, not only was John Joe a new councillor, he had obtained more votes than anyone else. The whole town laughed for a week. For the next year, John Joe attended every council meeting, not saying a word, just waiting for the issue of the trout farming to be raised— which it never was.

Closer to home was the older brother of Auntie May, Birdie. His real name was Patrick Griffin, although nobody ever used it. Birdie was a small, very thin man. He always wore a flat hat in or out of the house. In fact the only time he took it off was when he went to bed and upon entering church for Mass on a Sunday morning. He wore an overcoat that always seem to be about ten sizes to big

Birdie's prime task was to do the shopping, help around the house and also shop for old Mrs. Clancy, who lived in the Square.

I presume he got the name of 'Birdie' because when he was not whistling he was playing the mouth organ. He had a great collection of mouth organs. Uncle Andrew, when he came home from overseas, had always brought him a mouth organ from some part of the world. If you wanted to make Birdie happy then just buy him a mouth organ.

During the evenings, while everyone was doing the usual rounds of the neighbourhood with their ever-open doors, Birdie would finish mopping the kitchen and the hallway then just sit in the corner and play all the Irish airs. He was very talented and played his music with feeling.

Even though we shared a bedroom, Birdie hardly ever

spoke and appeared to not have an opinion on anything. Here was a quiet man with deep thoughts that he always kept to himself.

Birdie was a very private person. I once got a look at all his worldly goods that he kept in a case beneath his bed. In this case were a few pieces of jewellery kept in a tin box that he said belonged to his mother. He had a collection of circus posters that went back sixty years or more. Posters of Foster's Circus and Billy Smart's Circus, he was a wealth of knowledge on them and once took me to one as a child.

Birdie was first up in the morning and had the fire going for Auntie May when she got up, and with the tea already brewing. He would go down to the spout for the water, returning with two full buckets. We only drank water from the well (known as the spout), as that was considered pure. Tap water was for washing and cleaning.

One person I didn't like was Joe Hawes, unfortunately the only barber in town. The feeling was mutual as Joe did not like me either. I had two serious flaws that Joe hated with a vengeance. The first was that I was English and the second was my being a Protestant.

Willie would take me for a haircut and he had to drag me there all the way down Moore Street, past Joe Lynch's, Donnellan's Hardware and the post office to Joe's establishment.

Joe was a small man with a baldhead, tiny spectacles and a moustache. He had one barber's chair in his shop. He would put a piece of wood across the arms of the chair and sit me on it. He would then proceed to cut my hair and if I moved I got a belt across the head with a pair of scissors. Even if I did not move I still got a belt.

As if I did not know already, Joe would ensure that I was aware of his strong anti-British feelings that, in those days, lay deep in the heart of every Irishman and woman. The memories of what had happened, of the atrocities of the British army, the rapes, houses burnt and people tortured were still very fresh in people's minds in the forties. In the years that have passed since those days this attitude seems to have mellowed but I believe it is still not far below the surface.

To be fair, Joe was a man that had every right to hate the British because of what he had witnessed and endured at the hands of the Black and Tans. Joe, it was said, played a major role in the town and the county fighting the Black and Tans from 1917 through to independence in 1922. He was an active member of the I.R.A. and deep down the brutality that he had endured firsthand at the hands of these soldiers could not be forgotten. He was captured by the British, questioned, tortured and badly beaten. It is reputed that Joe had shot and killed three British soldiers during those years in Kilrush.

Joe was extremely proud of his nephew, Captain Tubridy, of the Irish army. He had a picture of him on the wall wearing his uniform, jumping over one of the fences during a Dublin horse show. Captain Tubridy was an international equestrian rider and represented Ireland. Tragically, Captain Tubridy was later killed in a jumping accident at the height of his fame.

I think Joe told most of his stories while I was having my haircut to ensure that I received the right education on British brutality and to let me know how he felt about the dreaded English. Joe ran the local reserve corps and they would meet in the Drill Hall in Frances Street. Willie was a member of this along with Joe O'Donnell and Johnny Enright. You would see Joe marching them down Frances Street of a summer's evening and out the Cappagh Road. Mind you, Joe did all his training from the saddle; he was always riding his bike.

Joe told the story of how they had killed a soldier out on the Cappagh Road and the British rounded up practically everyone and held them in The Square. They selected some people for interrogation and one boy was 15 years of age. He refused to tell them anything. They tied him to the back of a wagon and dragged him the 3 miles to Moyasta. He was a young innocent boy who knew nothing and he suffered a horrible death. Paddy O'Brien and Uncle Andrew confirmed this story. It was a good job for me that Auntie May and Uncle Andrew didn't share Joe's hatred for the English.

I was never happier though when a stranger arrived in town and opened a barber's shop next to Halpin's in Henry Street. He had one sure customer forever—me.

One funny thing sticks in my mind and it concerned the only garage in Kilrush. Tom Joe Reidy, known far and wide as Tom Joe, was the proprietor of this garage. It was located at the crossroads on the corner of Kilkee Road and Henry Street. The garage was next door to Keating's butcher shop, and just two doors away from Doyle's Bar, owned by Jack and Florrie Doyle. It wasn't a big garage, having just a single petrol pump, but everyone who owned a vehicle used it.

I was walking in town, just crossing The Square when someone told me that Tom Joe's garage was on fire. Together with a few others, I ran towards it. When I reached the garage, the fire was well established.

Now, being the only mechanic in Kilrush, it was one of Tom Joe's assignments to maintain the one fire truck possessed by the town. The fire station was close to his garage, being just one hundred yards away on the corner of Henry Street and Vandeleur's Street. When the fire was reported, the call had gone out for the firemen to attend the station. Tom Joe was the driver of the truck. He had climbed into the cab and turned the ignition. The truck would not start. Jumping down, the fireman tried to bump start it by pushing it. I tried to help them in this task. With Tom Joe at the wheel, we would heave the truck; get it moving until

it was fast enough for Tom Joe to let out the clutch—and…..
nothing.

By this time, others could see that the fire truck itself was in trouble. Unless the engine was running, the pump wouldn't operate. People started to run with buckets of water, but to no avail. The flames just climbed higher and higher.

In the meantime, someone made a call to the Ennis fire brigade, which was 20 miles away. By now the garage was well and truly ablaze with flames engulfing the whole place. The worry was about the petrol pump and the butcher's shop next door.

Eventually the Ennis fire brigade arrived and took control. We still continued pushing the Kilrush fire engine with Tom Joe still at the wheel but to no avail.

It's hard to explain how a fire engine from 20 miles away can beat a fire engine from 100 yards away but it did and it made the national newspapers.

Fortunately for Tom Joe, he was fully insured and a beautiful garage rose from the ashes of the old, one complete with a showroom. I bet that Tom Joe kept better care of the fire truck after that.

CHAPTER TWENTY TWO

Back To The Brothers

My teacher in the fifth year was Brother Walsh. When I first learned of this at first I thought that the sadistic bastard of my earlier years had returned from India. It was with great relief that I soon discovered that this was a young Brother Walsh. This was his first school and we were his first class. He was a very keen and eager teacher with all the enthusiasm that goes with a first assignment. Brother Walsh was very keen on homework. In fact he gave us so much that it was like going to school again when you arrived home. The following day, this very thorough Christian Brother checked all homework and if one had omitted even one assignment, he would cane you. No excuses were accepted and it was his standard that all homework would be completed, without exception. He was a very authoritarian type of Christian Brother who generally was fair. I only had a problem with him once. That was the occasion when Gerard and I went on the motorbike to Shannon Airport.

Gerard and I planned to go after tea to Shannon Airport to watch the planes and see the lights. In the early 1950s Shannon was the busiest airport in the world. All planes from Europe had to stop at Shannon to refuel for the long trip across the Atlantic to America. A refuelling was also required for those returning from the United States to Europe. The planes always came in the evening time and used to fly through the night to the USA.

The planes were the old Clippers, which unlike the jet aircraft of today, landed and took off so gracefully.

The end result of this particular visit to Shannon Airport was that no homework at all was done by me that night. The following day, as was usual, the teaching of various subjects was broken into periods. At each period, the first thing Brother Walsh would demand was that we hand in our homework for that particular subject. Each period, I had to confess to not having done my homework. Brother Walsh had his standards and his rules stated that you received four of the best for each subject you had not done. By lunchtime I had received twelve strokes of the cane on my hands. He gave me four for not having my English homework, then four more for not having my Irish homework and finally four more just before lunch for non-presentation of my religious homework.

When I went home for dinner my hands were very sore. Things did not change in the afternoon because I received another eight strokes of the cane, four for arithmetic and four more for geography. By the end of the day my hands were very, very swollen. Even though Brother Walsh could clearly see my hands were swollen it did not deter him from inflicting his stipulated punishment. The only time I think I ever really cried was after school on that day. On the way home I jumped the wall of the Convent Field opposite the handball alley and sat against the wall. My hands were red, swollen and so painful to touch. I sat in that field and cried for I don't know how long. There was no point in complaining to anyone, for these people could do no wrong, they were representatives of God.

The sixth-year was uneventful, we had Brother Gleeson back again and the familiarity was mutual. Most of this year was spent after the school in taking singing lessons. Brother Gleeson would keep me back after school and I would have to stand in the empty classroom and sing the scales. Brother Gleeson would pace up and down with his hands in his pocket's listening as I went through the scales, I had a slight lilt in my voice on occasions and he would get very annoyed if he heard it when I sang. Brother Gleeson was a tall, thin man with fiery red hair and a temper to match. During this year I had no problems with him. However some of the boys were not so lucky. He was cruel, brutal and could hand out punishment as good and as hard as anyone. Fortunately for me, my voice was my saving grace and maybe it was a year that was not so bad.

Summing up my years at school, I was, as were all boys in Kilrush, subjected to the brutality of a regime ruled by Christianity and Christian brothers. The people who ruled this education system were people of Christian religious beliefs but in truth were Satan's own people.

The Christian Brothers had the day-to-day responsibility of running the school. However, the overall indoctrination of the children of this parish of Kilrush was the responsibility of the Catholic Church.

The institutions of the Catholic Church in Kilrush consisted of the priesthood, The Christian Brothers, and the Sisters of Mercy. It was their responsibility and their responsibility alone to administer the education system to all children of the parish of Kilrush in a humane manner. These devils of religion failed in every way possible

Considering the abuse, the brutality and the inhumanity of this Christian society towards its children, both girls and boys, it is difficult to believe that such mental and physical brutality took place in that day and age.

There is nothing funny in meeting a Christian Brother, a person with long flowing gowns, a half collar around his neck, Rosary beads, a Bible and equipped with an armoury of weapons to inflict bodily pain in the name of Jesus Christ Almighty. His armoury was a leather strap, a Hawthorn stick with thorns cut off and if needed, a fist.

They believed and they acted on this earth as representatives of God. Surely God could not have been so brutal. The priests were no better for they condoned the actions of the Christian Brothers. They were well aware of these atrocities and the brutality that went on within the schools.

I have asked myself on many occasions since, how, in the name of God were these people allowed to be near children? I have many questions still today about the philosophy of this religious cult who ruled children by terror.

In hindsight, St. Patrick has a lot to answer for because he banished the snakes from Ireland and gave us the Irish Catholic Religion as it is today. I know he got things wrong. It would appear that he got rid of all the snakes in Ireland and left us children with the serpents (Christian Brothers). As far as I am concerned "give me the snakes any day."

The Currach
Builders

Our next-door neighbour was Marty Blunnie and Marty was a true fisherman. Marty made everything he needed to earn his living himself, including his own currach and nets. Marty's currach was a two-seater and easy to handle. I watched Marty build his currach from scratch. I watched as the frame slowly took form over days and weeks as he slowly but surely constructed the boat. I watched in amazement as he laid the canvas over the frame. He had a large bucket of coal tar and heated it over the fire. He then spread the coal tar all over the canvas with a big round brush. When he finished he had a magnificent boat.

Marty would do most of his fishing during the night in the sheltered waters at Brews Bridge and Scough Point. You would see him come home in the morning laden down with his nets over his shoulder and his catch of fish in a hessian sack.

Marty was a strong man of about 5 feet 8 inches tall, slim with thinning black hair. I can picture him now walking up the path with a big smile and carrying his bag of fish. He had a great smile and his face had that rugged look that we all had. He would wink at me as he passed. I used to "borrow" his currach. Marty knew it but he never let on. I used to row it out of the creek and over to Cappagh. Sometimes I would fish off the boathouse and catch the mackerel and whiting. Later on, Marty would lend me the boat because he knew I could handle it as he most probably saw me when he went up Frances Street on his way to the pub. I was about 12 years of age at this time. Marty liked his pint of stout and he most probably looked down the road, out into the creek and there I was as large as life, in his currach, fishing away near the old Customs House or boathouse.

Some say that the currach originates from the Aran Islands situated in Galway Bay. I would dispute that as I believe that the currach was taken to the islands from the mainland many hundreds, perhaps thousands of years ago. The Aran Islands are about 35 miles north west of Kilrush as the crow flies, off the Cliffs of Moher. On any day you can see the Aran Islands from the cliffs, unless there is a storm blowing, a regular occurrence. The ocean in this part of the world is unforgiving with seas that can be monstrous even on a good day.

The currach is made of tarred canvas stretched over a wooden frame, and although a very light structure it can ride out almost any size of wave. Great skill however is required to handle these boats properly, as many people over the years have found out to their peril.

These boats can be as large as twenty-five feet long with a four-foot beam, are cheap, easy to build, and very practical. They're also very light, so if you live in a place without a good pier or where you can't leave your boat in the water overnight, the currach can be lifted up by a couple of people and carried away. I could lift the fourteen-footer of my neighbour's boat on my own at 12 years of age and carry it down to the water.

The currachs were part of every day life on the West Coast of Ireland, not only for transportation, but also often for survival. In Kilrush, one could see lines of them down by the Customs House on the quay, over at the boathouse and out at Cappagh. This little craft could be seen everywhere around the waters edge and they were the lifeline of the islanders and the poor people of the town.

In Kilrush, Mike O'Brien was the professional currach builder and he built a lot of boats over the years.

Mike lived on the corner at The Cross, on the corner of Pella Road and O'Gorman Street. Mike was another one of those valuable people in the town, one of those very highly skilled people that no longer exist today. Mike used to play the malodeon in his spare time and he taught his son JP to play it also. John Patrick was called JP for short.

Mike was a great builder of currachs and he built three different kinds; the two, three and four-seaters. He also built variations. Some currachs were slim and fast, built for the pilot men at Scattery Island, while others were built for carrying goods like turf, food, house furniture etc. to the islands. These latter currachs were broader and much stronger than the normal currach. He had a great reputation for building the boats.

Mike would often be out at Doherty's sawmill, selecting the right wood for his currachs. Kilrush had two sawmills, Blunnies in Burton Street and Doherty's sawmill on the Cappagh Road. These were the only sawmills in County Clare and we had an ample raw timber supply, something that other areas of Clare did not have. Some people used to call them the Kilkee currach but Mike O'Brien made them all in Kilrush.

The fishermen from Kilkee, Carrigaholt, Scattery, Doonbeg and even Kerry had their currachs made by Mike and he used to make some changes to them to suit the different conditions. One refinement was the addition of a board; know locally as the bulwark, which enveloped the sides and stern, preventing nets from snagging. They were needed in the rough waters of the Atlantic Ocean.

In Mike's front garden you could see boats being constructed, all in various stages of completion. At the back of his house was a shed full of boats, with more stacked on top of the roof. Currachs would also be all over his back garden.

Patrick Scanlon, known locally as Pa, was the master currach builder and had taught Mike O'Brien among many others in the art of building the currach. He had worked on the old sailing ships and he was about 95 years old when he died in 1955, yet he was still building the odd currach here and there until the day he died.

Paddy lived on the opposite corner to Mike at the end of O'Gorman Street in a little cottage. He would often sit outside his little white cottage with its thatched roof, smoking an old clay pipe and telling us stories of far away places. He told us about all the sailing ships that came into Kilrush in the old days. Kilrush was the main port of western Ireland he said and we had a population of about 10,000 people. I wondered where all these people had lived?

He would tell us how the Customs House was full in those days and the sailing ships lined the quay. As a young lad of 12 years old he was taken on as a galley boy and told of how his first ship sailed from Kilrush to Liverpool and back.

He made some of the most beautiful model sailing boats you have ever seen. The model ships were so delicate, built with loving care and all with magnificent sails. He would tell us the stories of where he had sailed in all of these wonderful boats. Pa was a ship's carpenter in the old sailing ships. The model boats he made were all of boats in which he had sailed, but his pride and joy were his model currachs. These models were about eighteen inches long, displaying the whole range of currachs he used to build. If you wanted a currach built you picked from one on these models and sure enough Pa or Mike would make it for you. Even at the age of 90 he always had a currach under construction at the side of his cottage.

He was a master craftsman and thankfully he passed his skills on to Mike.

Pa reminded me of Popeye as he always wore a flat cap tilted on the side of his head, a shirt with no collar, a waist-coat and of course his trade mark the clay pipe. He used to make currachs in his younger days and he would tell of how Mike was his apprentice. He would give me three pence and I would have to go to Maude Griffin's shop with a jug for some Guinness, Maude would put a little extra in for him. He would sit on a stool outside his front door, relax in the sun and continue with his great tales of years gone by.

Fast Track To Catholicism

At the age of eleven it was decided that I become a Catholic. I have no idea who decided, when they decided or why they decided that I had to become Catholic. I presume it was Auntie May's decision and the family agreed that it was in my best interest to become part of the great Catholic family. According to Auntie May, I had to be able to enter heaven and Protestants, no matter how good they were, were not allowed into heaven.

Becoming a Catholic was a very hush, hush affair. Well it was a very hush, hush affair to me because I had no idea what was going on and I was the one that was becoming a Catholic. It all happened so fast that I'm not sure what time of the year it occurred. Nobody sat me down and told me what was about to happen, or to explain to me what being a Catholic meant. Mind you having lived in the Deloughery family's home since I was four years of age you would think I had a reasonable idea by then.

It started on a Friday afternoon when all those boys who were to be confirmed were marched from the school to the church. I was told I had to join them.

The church was right next door so we didn't have far to go. The event was to meet Bishop Rogers, the newly appointed Bishop of Clare. At the time he was the youngest bishop ever appointed in the Catholic Church. We all of us walked down the aisle of the church and sat on the right-hand side while the girls were sat on the left-hand side.

The church was beautifully decorated for this occasion, the confirmation of the young in our parish. The altar of St. Senan's Church is a thing of beauty. It is made of white marble and stood about 40 feet high. Behind the altar, reaching to the magnificent ceiling were three large stained glass windows. The centre pane was the figure of St. Senan in all his glory. The rail around the altar was also white marble, with each pillar beautifully carved. Two gates made of brass opened inwards.

Bishop Rogers sat in a high chair right between the two gates. He was dressed in red robes and he looked so magnificent sitting there surrounded by priests and Christian Brothers. The purpose of this exercise was for each boy and girl who was to be confirmed to go forward to the bishop and he would ask them simple questions on the Catechism and the Catholic faith.

I was so frightened; I thought that if he asked me my name I wouldn't have been able to tell him. Here was the Bishop of Clare in all his glory, surrounded by the priests and the Canon with the Christian Brothers and a few nuns thrown in for good measure. A more frightening situation for an eleven year-old boy or girl would have been hard to find. I suppose we could thank God that this occasion happened only every three years and thus there were a lot of children in the town to be confirmed.

By the time I got to Bishop Rogers I was a complete mess. He asked me some questions and I really don't know if I answered. He appeared to be more interested in who I was. Father Ryan spent some time explaining who this young boy was in front of him. "This is young Riley," explained Father

Ryan and he proceeded to tell him of my circumstances. I knelt before the bishop. He blessed me and I kissed the ring on his hand. All in all a very stressful situation for young Catholic let alone a Protestant. I suppose I was the first Protestant to do such things because as yet I had not been baptized a Catholic.

The only one that faltered at question time was a young lad from Moyasta who was not from my class and I suppose he was as frightened as anybody. Bishop Rogers asked this young lad, "Why is next Sunday so important to Catholics around here?" Well being honest I don't think I could have answered that because I was so frightened. However this particular genius, who was about one shilling short of a 10 bob note, looked totally bemused. A few seconds later I think the Holy Ghost descended on him like a bolt of lightning and a smile came over his face as he responded "My Lord. It is important because it's the horse races at Kilkee." A bemused look could be seen on Bishop Rogers face although there were no smiles on the faces of the Christian Brothers. The Christian Brothers were a bad lot and they did a lot of bad things, however I am sure if death by firing squad were allowed, that young boy would have been put against one of the gravestones outside the church and executed on the spot.

That same Friday evening, at about 9:30 p.m., I went to St. Senan's Church with Auntie May.

We were all dressed in our best clothes. I had on a grey suit; my jacket was handmade by Katie, short trousers with knee length stockings. I wore new black, lace-up shoes. I also wore a white shirt with a red tie. Sean, Willie, Gerard were all dressed in their best clothes as were Lulu and Mary. Johnny Enright and Katie, who were married by then, and Joe O'Donnell were present for my baptismal, a gathering of the people who cared for and loved me.

It seemed an odd time of night to be getting baptized,

however baptized I was to be. To tell the truth, judging the time of this ceremony, it would appear that I was highly privileged.

For young Joe Riley my goodness, there were three priests and the canon! Surely no child in Kilrush had ever had such a welcome into the Catholic faith or maybe it was because they did not trust this scallywag and wanted to make sure that I would not escape. The only one missing from this occasion was Bishop Rogers himself.

Father Ryan baptized me. The same Father Ryan I had known since I was very small boy. He was more of a friend than a priest and I believe that he had a lot to do with me being converted into the Catholic faith. This was the same Father Ryan that took me out to the islands to sing at his Mass and serve at the altar. I also sang many times as a young Protestant boy not many feet from where I was now to be baptized at the font. Brother Gleeson would have me singing the Ave Marie from the balcony, just above where we were. If the truth was known I had no idea of what it was all about, I was just there.

Father Ryan baptized me in the name of Jesus Christ and poured holy water on my head. Sean was my godfather and Katie was my godmother. I was so lucky to have such beautiful people by my side. The church had been closed for this special occasion and the only light was from the candles being held by the attendees. The candles lit up their faces. I could see how happy Auntie May was at the whole affair. I later learned that she had obtained my parents permission for me to go through this religious event. At that time of night it was so quiet and every little noise could be heard throughout the church. We said prayers, the Hail Mary and the Lord's Prayer. Father Ryan said a few words of welcome to God's church. The words echoed through the empty church, which appeared an eerie place in the dark.

The next events I suppose were funny in a way. I must

have set some new records in the history of the Catholic faith; if not in the Catholic faith then surely in the history of the Catholic religion of Kilrush Parish. Within five minutes of being baptized, Father Conneady took me to a confessional box so that he would hear my first confession.

I was so nervous. I'm sure that Father Conneady was not in the mood for a confession from one of the biggest rascals of the town. Considering I was about eleven years of age, Father Conneady may have been there until morning listening to my sins, so he saw fit to forgive me all of my sins and gave me absolution, with a penance of three Hail Mary's and the Lord's Prayer.

I came out of the confession box knelt down and said my penance, the candles on the altar were lit and it was a very quiet and solemn place. Auntie May waited just outside the door of the church and as I came out, she gave me a kiss and so did Katie, Lulu and Mary. Then the newly born Joseph Senan Riley accompanied them home.

The next morning I went to 8 o'clock mass and we went to the front row of seats in the church. Father Flynn gave me my first Holy Communion. I had my best clothes on and the Reverend medal and ribbon that one wears on the collar of the jacket when making the first Holy Communion. All of this happened in the presence of the family, Auntie May, Willie, Sean, Gerard, Mary, Katie, Lulu and Birdie.

When we got home there was at beautiful breakfast laid out on the table as Kaybe from next door had helped in setting it up while we were at Mass. This was the occasion of my first Holy Communion and the Communion breakfast that goes along with it. This is the Irish tradition for someone receiving his or her first Communion.

Auntie May was so happy as were all of the family. We all sat around the table and for the first time everyone sitting at the table for this very special breakfast, was a Catholic. It was only on rare occasions that the white cloth came out on the table, occasions such as Christmas, Easter or when one of the priests or nuns came to visit. All the family members as well as the neighbours gave me cards and usually there was money in most of them. I remember Mrs. Corbett coming across and she was always very good to me. Often she would put her hand on my head, shake my hair and give me a kiss, at the same time saying "poor crater" as she smiled with a tear in her eyes.

I had spent a lot of time in Mrs. Corbett's house because Senan, her son, was my best friend. Senan was the only friend I ever had at school and one that never once saw anything but me. He never saw religion or the country of my birth as an obstacle to a friendship. Most friends in school at one time or another would mention my religion or my nationality in a derogatory manner at some stage, but never Senan. We sat next to each other in school, shared the same stool, shared the same desk, often shared our homework and played together. Senan was smaller than me, a little bit tubby (he would kill me for saying that) but a more loyal or better friend was hard to find. I first met Senan as a four or a five-year-old boy. At this time Senan lived down the lane in a little cottage and we played very simple games. When they built the new houses up in Pella Road, Mrs. Corbett got the last house up on the right-hand side. Senan moved there when he was about eight. The family moved back about a year later and lived across the road.

So this Saturday was an eventful day for me. In less than twelve hours I had been baptized, had my first confession and received Holy Communion.

That evening I was playing and along the road I could see walking towards me Bishop Rogers, Father Flynn, Father Ryan and Father Conneady. They were walking up the centre of the road with their robes flowing in the breeze, wearing their hats. It was a beautiful evening with the sun setting behind them in the heads as they walked up Pound Street. Looking back on it the scene reminded me of the last part in the film "My Darling Clementine" and the fight at the OK Coral when Henry Fonda as Wyatt Earp and his three brothers walk down the street to face the Clampet's.

When they got to our house, Father Ryan called me and introduced me again to Bishop Rogers. In the middle of the road he held out his hand and I knelt down to kiss the ring on his hand.

"This is young Riley," said Father Ryan.

"Yes." answered the bishop. "I remember him."

"He was baptized last night, your Grace," said Father Ryan.

"Yes," said the bishop. "I remember you told me about him over dinner."

"Yes, your Grace." said Father Ryan.

"Can we meet the good lady who has looked after him?" asked the bishop.

"Yes." said Father Ryan. "She lives just here."

"It would be nice to meet with such a good woman," observed the bishop

"This way," said Father Ryan.

With this they all went through the gate, up the path and into the house. Auntie May nearly had a heart attack. For here in all of his glory was the Bishop of Clare standing in our kitchen with three priests. She was beside herself and didn't know what to do. This was the first time that a bishop had walked down the street of our part of town let alone walked into a house. A crowd gathered outside and they were all wondering what was going on. Bishop Rogers and the priests sat down to have a cup of tea. It was served in the bone china that was kept for very special occasions. Auntie May had to explain the extraordinary circumstances surrounding of how this young Protestant boy arrived in Kilrush. To give them their due they were very interested in my spiritual well-being and my story.

The bishop praised Auntie May for all she had done. Auntie May knelt down with Katie and he blessed them both. Before he left he gave Auntie May a set of Rosary beads that he had in his pocket. These Rosary beads were her prize possession for years and I have them in my possession today.

On Sunday morning we were all up early for this very special day in the town of Kilrush, the day of my Confirmation. Willie spent some time with me before I went to church. However I always had great difficulty in taking anything that Willie said seriously. He started talking very seriously and I laughed. This was usually the point when he would say "this is not a laughing matter" and clip me on the ear, which only made me laugh more. He would then get very serious and say "Boyyo I will kick your arse if you don't listen to me." Auntie May would intervene and protect me saying "leave the poor crater alone."

Here was Willie (our local radio station) lecturing me on the virtues of Confirmation and all of this was already beyond me. It was impressed upon me that, according to Willie, a great change was about to befall me. He said the Holy Ghost would descend upon me and I would receive some great gifts such as understanding, wisdom, knowledge and of course fear of the Lord. At this point I knew that his imagination had run away with him or he was serious and expecting some kind of miracle from above.

This had been a great weekend also for Senan Corbett and Paddy Enright because of the small cash gifts that were given to us. Especially in my case because I had a double whammy, it was like a winning the local Bingo that was held in the school hall on Thursday nights. I had money from my first Communion on Saturday as well as my Confirmation on Sunday. We all went down to Maude Griffin's shop, purchased a packet of cigarettes, and availed ourselves of every opportunity to hide behind one of the headstones in the churchyard to have a smoke.

All in all it was a great occasion and one that I would not have missed for the world. It was important that it made people happy. I was happy because Auntie May was so proud of me and so was all of the family. I think Auntie May was happy because I was now a fully-fledged Catholic and the best part was that I could now enter heaven.

This had been fast track Catholicism at its best, baptism, confession, first communion and confirmation, all in less than 48 hours.

CHAPTER TWENTY FIVE

A Grand Sight

It was one of those rare summer days in Kilrush. There was not a breeze, the day was warm and for once, the waters of the Atlantic Ocean were like a millpond. It being Sunday, Sean suggested we take a currach and go fishing. Gerard agreed to go with us.

Together, Sean and I smoothly took the boat through the water to within half of a mile off Scattery Island in line with Scough Point. When we arrived at our destination, I took over the oars in order to gently row while Gerard trawled for fish from the stern. Sean sat in the bow, laid back smoking a cigarette and just enjoying the weather.

We were fishing in the traditional way, using hand-lines. Most currachs carried two hand-lines. These were wound around a three-foot length of timber that was termed a "sally rod." Each rod held about 120 feet of hemp line and a lead weight of about six ounces was secured 12 feet from the end of the line. If lead weights were not available, a suitable stone would be picked up from the shore and used instead. Firmly attached to the line was about 6 feet of finer hemp called the "snoud." Attached to the snoud was a swivel then a final six feet of "gut." Progress replaced the gut with nylon of about 30 pounds breaking strain. This allowed fish of up to 10 pounds to be hauled in without having to play them.

It was a peaceful day. Gerard had both lines out, a hand on each ready to detect any bite. Sean continued to relax in the bow while I slowly moved the oars through the water with hardly a splash. Occasionally I would glance over my shoulder to check where we were heading. I had taken a quick check when my head swivelled back again. I had thought I had seen a hump in the water.

"Sean," I said. "What's that up ahead?"

Sean sat up and turned to the bow. "Where, Joe?" he asked.

"Up there," I replied. "In the water, toward Carrigaholt."

"I can't see a thing," answered Sean. Hearing the conversation, Gerard had stood up in the stern. "It looks like a shoal of fish," he said.

I stopped rowing so that I could turn to have a better look. "It must be a big shoal," I said. "Will you look at that? The water is alive."

"What do you think they are?" asked Gerard.

By now Sean could also see them. "They look like porpoise to me," he said. I later learned that though always known as porpoises locally, these were in fact Bottlenose Dolphins.

Suddenly, I didn't like it a bit. "Porpoise?" I shouted. "Are you sure?"

"Let's get the hell out of here," said Gerard, rapidly pulling in the lines.

The beauty of the afternoon seemed to disappear suddenly. Coming right at us, travelling very fast, was a pod of about one hundred dolphins. We were in the wrong place and certainly in the wrong sort of boat to get caught in the middle of their mad rush. We could see the water was alive as it got closer and closer to us.

"Sean," shouted Gerard, desperately winding in lines. "Will you get rid of that fokkin cigarette and get to rowing?"

Alone at the oars, I started to panic. "We'd better be quick," I said. "They will be on top of us in a minute."

The panic must have suddenly lifted Sean's usual inability to row well. Pulling together we could have won the Olympics. We headed for the safety of Scattery Island and as soon as I could see the kelp and rocks below us, I knew we were okay and I breathed a sigh of relief.

It was a grand sight though as we sat in the currach and watched this huge pod pass us by. We watched them head down towards Hog Island and then carry on up the River Shannon. It took nearly twenty minutes for them all to pass us.

"I've seen a lot of porpoise in my time," commented Sean. "But never have I seen so many in one pod."

"I wonder where they came from?" asked Gerard.

"They are probably following the mackerel or salmon," said Sean.

"Well," observed Gerard. "That's the end of today's fishing. If there had been anything out there, it will be gone now for sure."

"That was close," I said, awed with the sight, but realizing we had had a close thing.

"It was too close for comfort," said Sean. I was glad he had been scared too.

It is not as though the dolphin would harm us in any way but they don't know that the currach is made from lathes and canvas. Dolphins love to play with boats and that's fine when there are only one or two of them, but a pod would be dangerous.

A pod normally consists of about 30 to 40 or so dolphins. I had never seen these many before, about 100 dolphins. It was a magnificent sight to see but not to be in the middle of them in a canvas boat. When there are so many there are always those that want to play. There favourite trick is to come at the boat from the stern at speed, just before they get to the boat they turn over on their belly and rub it on the bottom of the boat. That's okay in a wooden clinker built boat or a ship, but not in a canvas boat.

We chatted for a while. The afternoon was so quiet, no wind or ripple on the water that our voices sounded unnaturally loud.

"Do you think they have gone?" asked Sean.

"I don't think it wise to move just yet," answered Gerard.

"They might be coming up the back of Hog," I said.

"No," said Sean. "I think they will be well up river by now."

"Well. Let's get going and get home," decided Gerard.

"We will head for Scough Point and go in from there," said Sean.

"Riley." said Gerard. "Come on Boyyo. Let's get moving."

Gerard was always the boss and what he said went. "There is only one captain here," said Gerard, with a laugh. "That's me"

"Yeah," I answered. "And didn't someone say the same thing on the Titanic?"

"Okay, smart arse," said Sean. "Let's get rowing."

As we rowed across to the point we were wary and kept a close watch for any signs of the dolphin's return. My hands were beginning to get sore at the rate we were rowing as we were in a hurry to get into the creek and to safety.

At Benediction that evening, I knew what both Sean and Gerard were thanking the Lord for that day. They were not alone.

Chapter Twenty Six

The Love Boat

Kilrush could be considered by some as an 'end of the line' town. Unlike Ennis or Limerick, we weren't on the road to anywhere in particular. However, being a port, albeit small, we were reminded that somewhere over the horizon there was a world out there by the occasional ship putting in to our town. This would happen perhaps seven or eight times a year. The ships would either be delivering timber or loading flour from Glynn's flourmill for Europe. A visit by a ship was a cause for not only excitement, but was an opportunity for a few days work to many unemployed men. We were always the first to know of an impending visit as Katie's husband, Johnny Enright was the head of the stevedores union, and his duty was to recruit the necessary manpower.

Johnny had told us that a ship bringing a load of timber for Doherty's sawmill was due to arrive. Small vessels could be brought right into the Creek, but the one expected was about 15,000 tons and would have to dock at the Cappagh pier.

On a lovely spring evening, myself, Katie and Lulu accompanied Johnny to the pier. We could see the ship anchored in the Scattery Roads waiting for high tide. The pilot from Scattery Island was already on board when they lifted the anchor. The pilot guided the ship up the river on the Kerry side, then cut across at Killimer into the deep water channel close to Hog Island, before bringing it alongside the pier.

Once the ship was tied up and the gangplank in place, our local custom's officer, together with Johnny, went aboard. We stood waiting patiently while the formalities were being completed. The custom's officer, over a few bottles of beer of unknown origin, would clear the ship, while Johnny would seek out the ships 3rd officer to plan the unloading.

It was not long before Johnny appeared at the rail and waved to us to go on board. As soon as we reached the deck, Johnny introduced us to the 3rd officer whose name was Hans Jensen. Hans was from Denmark and very Scandinavian in appearance. He was five feet nine inches tall, fair skin, blonde hair and blue eyes. He took us all to the officers' mess and gave us coffee and chocolates. Unfortunately, Hans could speak only a little English, but his eyes spoke a great deal as he kept his gaze on Lulu. Few of us noticed that Lulu appeared mesmerised by Hans. We stayed in the mess for about an hour and then Hans insisted on accompanying us on the walk home.

It is a true saying that familiarity breeds contempt. I had been an infant when I entered the Deloughery household, and Lulu had been just a slip of a colleen, the baby of the family. I had not noticed that she had become a petite and good-looking young lady of nineteen. She had the typically Irish dark hair but vivid blue eyes, and a 'peaches and cream' complexion. Lulu had also developed the Deloughery sense of humour and was always quick with a smile. It is little wonder then, that on our journey home, Hans just couldn't keep his eyes from her.

The following morning, all was ready to start the unloading. The West Clare Railway had a station at Cappagh Pier. The line ran through the station and ended at a set of buffers that were close to the slipway. The pier itself was at right-angles to the railway line, but a set of tracks ran the length of the pier. A hand-operated turntable allowed goods wagons to be stationed alongside a ship. The empty wagons would be parked either in the station itself or in an adjacent siding on the day prior to unloading. An engine would select a wagon and shunt it onto the turntable. A gang of men would physically turn the wagon to line up with the rails on the pier and then push it to its required position alongside the ship.

Once the wagon was fully loaded, the services of Jack Hanrahan would be employed. His council work had to be abandoned for a few days and his cart left behind. Instead, a large collar was fitted to the horse with two long chains attached. With a little help from the men, the horse would drag the now heavy wagon back to the turntable where it would be realigned with the main track. The horse would then drag it along the spur to the buffers. Once there were a number of fully loaded wagons, the engine would then take them from the pier directly into Doherty's sawmill for unloading. Of course, if flour was being loaded for export, the process would be reversed. During these times, the pier was a hive of activity. The work was hard, the hours long, but the money it put into the pockets of the men employed was very welcome.

I don't know when it happened, but at some time during their initial meeting of the previous evening, Lulu had promised to meet with Hans. She had to tell me, of course, because I was to be the excuse for her "taking the air."

"Don't you be breathing a word of this, Riley. If you do and my ma finds out, sure and I'll kill you myself, so I will," she said. "Mention one word about Hans, I promise. I'll kill you."

"Hans who?" I nonchalantly replied. Lulu seemed to forget that it was not that too long ago I had done the same thing for when Katie wanted to meet Johnny. I was an expert at this type of subterfuge, although I wasn't sure if Hans would know he was supposed to pay me sixpence a time. I just hoped Lulu would inform him of this local custom.

That evening, after she had returned from her job in the Monastery, Lulu disappeared to her bedroom. When I had finished my tea, I went to the bottom of the stairs and shouted up loud enough for Auntie May to hear, "Lulu. I'm going out for a walk. Would you be wanting to join me?"

"Just a minute, Joe. I'm just combing my hair, then I'll come with you," a voice shouted back. "Will that be okay, ma?"

"Where are you going?" asked Auntie May.

"Probably up around the Square," I answered. "Just to see who is around." It was obvious that Auntie May was making no connection to the fact that a ship was docked at Cappagh. Lulu came to the top of the stairs. She looked stunning. She had on a dress I hadn't seen before, her hair was immaculate and she looked a million dollars. If Auntie May saw her dressed up like this, the cat would have been out of the bag for sure. Lulu knew this as well as she signalled me to check on Auntie May's location. I casually strolled into the kitchen, pretending to look for something. Auntie May had settled into her favourite chair. I walked to the bottom of the stairs and signalled Lulu, who came rapidly down the stairs. We shot out of the front door, down the path and out of the gate. We quickly crossed the road and rounded the corner at the house of Mrs. Corbett, rapidly walking down the lane until we were sure to be out of sight. We then slowed the pace and enjoyed our walk out to Cappagh Pier. We chatted a bit although Lulu's mind seemed preoccupied.

Hans was anxiously leaning on the rail of the ship when we got there and he came hurriedly down the gangway to the pier and greeted Lulu. Johnny said hello and gave a big smile, a wink and a nod of approval to Lulu. This was the usual time for Joe to get lost again with or without sixpence and do something until it was time to go home. I decided I would stay with Johnny as he continued to unload the ship into the late evening.

Lulu and Hans went for a walk out past Ryan's house to Aylevaroo. This happened for the next three days until the ship left.

We walked out to Cappagh in the evening of the fourth day and Hans and Lulu said their good-byes on the pier, a sad occasion for them both. By now Lulu was madly in love with her handsome prince who came in on the Love Boat.

We watched, as the ship left the pier and Lulu was in tears as we stood there waving goodbye. We stayed and watched the ship sail into the sunset, out between the heads and into the Atlantic Ocean.

It was impossible for Lulu to keep her budding romance secret, because after that our postman, Michael Corbett, was kept constantly busy delivering letters addressed to Lulu bearing stamps from all over the world. As soon as one was delivered, Lulu would grab it and run up the stairs to her bedroom where she would sit on her bed reading and re-reading every one of them.

Some of these letters organised a telephone conversation. On the appointed day and at the hour agreed, Lulu would be waiting outside of the one public telephone box in the Square. This little green telephone box was the contact point between the citizens of Kilrush and their friends and relatives scattered all over the world. At the appointed hour, Hans would put a call through to the box and Lulu would dive inside to breathlessly answer it. Hans would call from all over; Spain, Denmark, the U.S.A., wherever his ship had docked.

In one letter, Hans told Lulu that he had some leave due to him and he wanted to use it to visit her in Kilrush. A conference was held with Auntie May as inquisitor. To everybody's surprise, Auntie May appeared to fully accept Hans as a possible suitor for Lulu, and not only agreed with him visiting, but suggested he stay in the house.

His holiday was a bigger success than anyone could have dreamed. He had been writing and telephoning for over a year, during the course of which he had been studying English. He had to speak slowly, and sometimes he got his grammar mixed, but at least we could talk with him. He had brought his camera and used it extensively around the town and on the many trips he and Lulu took. Towards the end of his holiday, he sat in the kitchen, and in halting English asked Auntie May for the hand of Lulu. To everybody's surprise, Auntie May agreed. She could see that they were totally in love with each other, but more importantly, she respected Hans. She could see that he was a gentleman in every respect, very strong minded and a traditionalist. He didn't drink or smoke.

As they were engaged, the second request, which was also approved, was that Lulu accompanies him to Denmark in order to meet with his family. Arrangements were made, the services of Gerald Griffin contracted, and off they both went covered in liberal sprinklings of Holy Water.

One year later, Hans returned to Kilrush together with his brother, who was to be his best man. They stayed down the road with Johnny and Katie. Hans had agreed to convert to Catholicism, so Father Ryan again came to the rescue and organised another fast-track conversion on behalf of the Deloughery family.

Came the day of the wedding. The only difficulty was explaining to Hans as to why he and his wedding party had to go down the lane to Frances Street in order to not see the bride. He was most anxious to meet with Lulu, but with a shrug, he eventually was persuaded to accept this Irish custom.

Our wedding party proceeded to the church the usual way. We walked up Pound Street, past the handball alley; turned right into Toler Street, past the Christian Brothers school and into St. Senan's Church. It was a beautiful Saturday morning with the sun blessing us all. Mary, Lulu's other sister, was her bridesmaid. Lulu was smiling and obviously so excited.

Lulu came down the aisle dressed in a perfect pink dress lovingly made for her by her sister, Katie, on the arm of Gerard, who, as Uncle Andrew was no longer with us, assumed the position of head of the family. I sat holding hands with Auntie May. We were happy and sad, happy to see Lulu marrying such a grand fellow as Hans, but sad because Uncle Andrew wasn't with us to see it.

As Father Ryan said the Mass and conducted the wedding ceremony, the solemnity was occasionally broken by the loud chatter of Joseph, the two-year-old son of Katie and Johnny.

While we were all at the church, the very good friends of the Deloughery family, Sue Morrissey, Cissie Roughan and Kaybe Blunnie were busy preparing the wedding breakfast.

We all enjoyed the wedding breakfast, and after it was time for the honeymoon. Unlike in many other countries, the Irish are not content with tying a few cans to a vehicle's fender and waving the happy couple farewell from outside of the venue of the reception. No way. The Irish like to make sure the couple arrive safely at their honeymoon destination. Thus, the services of Gerald Griffin and one other were sought, and two cars proceed in tandem to Galway. A bemused Hans was being introduced to yet another local tradition.

The party had a bit of excitement on the way. Just before we arrived in Lahinch the cars stopped as we had spotted a pod of whales about 300 yards off shore. The pod consisted of about a dozen killer whales, a beautiful sight to see and we watched them for about ten minutes as they swam past. When we arrived at the hotel in Galway we all went into the restaurant and had a cup of tea before making the return journey home.

Sean was the only one that stayed behind in Katie's house with a few other guests having a wedding drink. This was the day he really blotted his copybook. Sean, a person who for all intent and purposes did not drink at all, got a bit tipsy. He also gave some drink to little Joseph and the baby was also a bit tipsy. Katie was not amused and hit the roof. We all laughed about it later and I don't think Sean ever took another drink.

Hans and Lulu settled in Denmark, where they had five sons and a daughter. Such was the love of Hans for Lulu that he gave up international seafaring and became the first officer of a car ferry that travelled between Puttgarten in Germany and Rodby in Denmark. This allowed him to be home every two days.

Hans not only loved Lulu very much, but also Kilrush. He had planned for himself and Lulu to live in Kilrush once he retired. They had packed and shipped their personal effects and furniture, but on the very day he retired, Hans died. In accordance with his wishes, however, Lulu brought his body to Kilrush and buried him in New Shanakyle cemetery, in a spot overlooking the Shannon Estuary and the islands.

Lulu did live in Kilrush for a few years, taking care of Willie and Andrew until they too passed away, after which she returned to Denmark to be near her children.

I have little doubt that Lulu, like all Irish women, would have occasionally prayed to St. Jude for a loving husband. St. Jude not only answered her prayers, but found someone from far across the sea. If you do not believe in the power of St. Jude after this, then there is little hope for you.

CHAPTER TWENTY SEVEN

The Joys Of Being Catholic

For me Catholicism appeared very strange to say the least, but somehow it was also very practical within Kilrush society. It appeared that everything in life was centred on the Church. The Church was represented by the priests who spoke the word of God, and therefore had to be obeyed.

I believe that in Ireland, the trust in the priests is a deep-rooted situation that has developed over the centuries. We are talking about centuries of oppression and brutal suppression by British sovereignty. Throughout the centuries the Irish people had no rights. Not even the right to read or write English. The priests therefore had a position in society that was elevated because their voice was the only voice that the common people had.

Maybe the priesthood lost its way somewhere in those years because they ruled by fear; certainly not for the love of us and certainly not by the love of God.

We were taught that God ruled his people through his priests, but his priests ruled by the Catechism we were taught in school. The Catechism was there to continually remind us of how depraved a society we all were, and all because some clown took a bite of an apple a few thousand years ago. This idiot named Adam took a bite of an apple that was forbidden to him and the Lord God, in all his wisdom, decided that everybody of all nations should from then on be punished.

When you look back at the 1940s and 1950s, it was more like the dark ages than the twentieth century. What were these priests thinking of? It was considered to be a mortal sin to read your stars in a newspaper, to have your palm read and God help anybody who read tea leaves, they were doomed forever. Poor Sue Morrissey, one of our neighbours, practically made a living from reading tea leaves. According to the Church, Sue was doomed even though she was a very religious person.

We were also warned against reading certain books, magazines, some novels and anything that contained immodesty. I am not sure if the Beano or Dandy fitted into that category; as if it did then Sean and I were gone forever to the fires of hell.

And God forbid that anybody told a lie, for to tell a lie was considered to be outrageous and God's punishment for lying was an eternity condemned in hell.

When I look back at the situation, I believe that Paddy Griffin was the only person that I met who gave some logic to all this religion. He made out that God was a human being and understood slight misdemeanours and had a sense of humour to boot. I think he had more understanding of God than the priests did.

For even slight misdemeanours like holding hands with a girl or, worse still, sitting in the back row of the Mars Cinema on Saturday afternoon having a gentle smooch were considered bad and sinful. The Church never recognized the beauty and innocence of youth. We were very young, very innocent and maybe not so beautiful. However we were young people who did no more wrong than generations before us and generations that will follow us after we've left this earth. We were made to believe that God was extremely harsh and handed out punishment for such simple misde-meanours that we were fearful in every way. I can never remember a priest standing in church and preaching to a congregation saying, "God loves you."

As I said previously, the second most important thing at our end of town was money but the first thing was to avoid going to hell. It appeared that hell was uppermost in people's minds and the saying, "You will go to hell" was the normal way of keeping us in line. To speak against the established authority or to speak with contempt or disrespect against the priests, Christian Brothers or nuns in these times meant a scolding from your peers. Such people were held in high reverence and could do no wrong. This was evident by the treatment of boys and girls by the Christian Brothers and the nuns. The penalties handed out by these religious people were extreme to say the least, and yet I can never remember one parent going to the school to make a complaint.

I had great difficulty in understanding God and his Church for I could see very little humanity in any of it. If you go to this small town of Kilrush, you will see first hand the opulence of the Church. Kilrush had only a small popu-lation yet here were some of the most magnificent buildings that you could see anywhere on the West Coast of Ireland. St. Senan's Church is equal in beauty, size, architecture and its stained-glass windows as any cathedral in Ireland. The Convent was a magnificent piece of architecture with mani-cured gardens. The size of it was extreme for such a small, impoverished town.

The living quarters for the priests, Christian Broth-ers and the nuns certainly did not advertise poverty. The Church was very wealthy and owned the best real estate in the town. That is a fact that is worldwide when you see the real estate that is owned by the Church.

The priests had a real funny way of interpreting God's laws about what we should and should not do. For instance, to people who were married and the words they would say too them from the pulpit. The priests condemned all human life that was expressed sexually and it appeared that they just did not care about people and their feelings. It was apparent that my God seemed to me a harsh God who was void of any human feelings. The priests and the Christian Brothers moved around the community and I cannot remember seeing them smile or be happy, they were miserable beings that lived miserable gloomy lives.

The priests took a personal interest in each and every person in the town, especially in our district. Maybe it was because we were not considered to be as good as the richer people of town. Father Conneady was a hard man and had very little sympathy for anyone. His idea was that he was responsible to God for us all, and he was determined in his way that if he had to wallop us all the way into heaven, then he would do it.

All priests kept an eye on the young people of the town and, that included me, because the sins of the flesh i.e. sex, was the road to hell and the priests were determined to make sure that we walked a righteous path to heaven.

The Jesuit priests used to come once a year for the retreat. The retreat was an almighty, thunderous affair that preached hellfire and brimstone. The retreat lasted two weeks, one for the women and one for the men. The first week was always for the women and they went to church at 7:30 each evening for the service, the highlight of which was the sermon.

These priests were experts in the administration of psychological fear. I used to think years later, as I still do today, that these priests were the inventors of psychological warfare and it was they who used to train the Americans and the Russians.

The sermons that they gave had nothing to do with humanity, with a love of your fellow man or the community. The sermons that they gave were so precise and so vivid that if they were made today into films they would be X rated. No boy or girl under the age of 18 years should have been allowed into the church with these priests.

They had terrifying sermons on death and they gave real frightening descriptions on the many ways in which you could die. By the time you had finished with these people you believed you were going to die in a horrible manner and what's more you were going to die that night when you went home in your bed.

When you went home it was hard to go to sleep and for God's sake don't put the light out. I had bad dreams with all of this stuff.

They would also give you a great rendition of the Judgment Day. How we are all going to be up there, millions of us in this valley and judged by God. He was going to be a busy man so we had better behave ourselves.

I thought about it afterwards because you do think about these things. I had terrible impressions of it all and how they were going to manage all of these people up there. The angels would be flying all over the place, people wanting to go to the toilet, having to keep the men separated from the women because God was there and men and women could not be together. People would be using the public phones and mobile phones trying to get through to friends and relatives. When you called heaven this lady with an American accent would say, "Welcome to heaven. Press 1 for St. Peter. Press 2 for Gabriel. Press 3 for the saints. Press 4 for any angel and please note that you can get through to God any time because he's always listening."

The description of hell was equally as bad because Satan had an influx of millions and he was so busy shovelling hot coals on them, beating them and torturing them. It appears it is a busy time for everybody except those in heaven because not many made it up there.

After these sermons, each night the priests would hold confession. The confessional boxes were pretty full on these evenings, especially after the frightening description of hell and many have had to wait quite some time to have their confession heard. The best description that one could give to the confessional box at this time was, "the confessional box is a fire escape for all Catholics." The purpose of this retreat was to pull us into line and make sure that we behaved ourselves for the next twelve months. In my case it took about two days to return back to normal.

Our own priests were much gentler individuals than the Jesuit priests. Our priests main aims were, of course, to ensure that there was no population explosion, hence the sermons on sex and secondly, the sermons on money.

Following the sermons on sex and fornication came the usual demands for money. Not many people at our end of town had a great deal of money. In fact they were very poor. However it was considered that everybody gave what he or she could afford to support these righteous people. The priests in there own way believed that they were right and what they did was in the name of God. Their role was to tender to God's flock. Unfortunately this little flock might have been a little different to other parts of the world. Other parts of the world did not have a Paddy Griffin, a Jack Hanrahan or a Willie Deloughery to contend with. Not that you had to contend with these people because they were great people and I am sure that God would not forsake them.

When I look back at all of these sermons and how they were pitched to the congregation you could only interpret it in this manner, that if you were very wealthy and important your chances of getting into heaven were really good. The contrast to that was our end of town, we had no money and there were children everywhere so we had no chance.

On one occasion in the year the priest would read out

a list of people who had given money throughout the year. Not many people from our end of town made that roll of honour.

My interpretation of this exercise was that God preferred the rich and powerful to the poor. The clergy he selected as his servants demonstrated this point at every possible point. They lived a miserable existence, prophesied gloom and doom then tried to make our lives similar.

Just once, as a boy, I joined the ladies on one of their pilgrimages to Knock, County Mayo. It was one of the longest days in my life. It would have been also the most boring day of my life had it not been for Gerry Mahoney. Gerry was the engine driver on the West Clare Railway and he was related to the Deloughery family. Gerry was a small man who was a little portly. Gerry was married with children and he lived in the first new house on the right-hand side of Pella Road. He was always smiling and was a quiet man who kept to himself. Jerry had worked on the West Clare Railway all his life starting work at the station. Later, he was promoted to fireman and ended his days as the last driver of the West Clare Railway.

The West Clare Railway had their engine shed located down at the dock behind Mrs. Black's house and close to the seaweed factory. I sometimes went with Gerry on Saturdays as he did the short run to Kilkee and back. At Moyasta Junction the engine would be unhooked and the engine would go around the triangle and connect to the other end of the carriages.

Whilst this was going on, it was always a good excuse for anybody to pop into Taylor's bar. Sometimes the train would be late due to people not wishing to leave the bar. Gerry in his quiet way would have a very quick jar or two before we would head off to Kilkee. The same policy prevailed on the way back. Gerry was never in a hurry to get home. His fireman was a lad called John Carroll and he lived across the road from Gerry. When the train pulled into Kilrush it was John's job to check all the carriages for any property left behind with the Guard.

The carriages of the West Clare railway were the most unusual carriages on any railway in the world. Underneath the seats in the carriages (and remember this is a narrow gauge railway) there were heavy concrete blocks. As Gerry once explained to me, the reason for this was because of the high winds that came off the Atlantic coast. There was no protection from the winds as trees were few and far between. The landscape was generally barren, often covered with bogs and scraggy open country. They used the concrete blocks in the carriages as ballast to keep the train on the tracks. This little train traversed some of the most hostile country in the west of Ireland. From Moyasta Junction to Ennistymon was open country with nothing to stop the treacherous weather that the Atlantic Ocean is renowned for at any time of the year.

Kilrush owed much of its economic existence to the West Clare Railway. From Kilrush the trains travelled, north through Moyasta Junction, Doonbeg, Craggaknock, Kilmurry, Mullagh, Quilty, Miltown Malbay, Lahinch, Ennistymon, Willbrook, Corofin, Ruan and terminated at Ennis. The last train ran in 1964 and I feel sure that Kilrush lost a jewel with its passing. The West Clare Railway had been in existence for 100 years. They made quite a few films on that train. One such film was "The Rising of the Moon," with the famous Irish comedian Jimmy O'Dea and another was "A Minute's Wait" with Maureen Potter, Jimmy O'Dea and Barry O'Donovan.

As a result of my years with Gerry on the West Clare Railway, I learnt a lot about steam engines and when I went to England as a young boy of 16 years, I joined British Rail as a an engine cleaner at Aintree sheds in Liverpool. As an engine cleaner, I was used as a fireman on the steam trains when they were short of firemen. I qualified as a fireman in 1959, transferred to Neasden Sheds, London and worked on the express trains between London and York; all thanks to Gerry's training on the West Clare Railway.

On that particular day, the West Clare Railway was to get a baptism by pilgrims. Gerry Mahoney had a timetable to keep that did not allow him to have a jar along the way, well at least not until he got to Ennis. The pilgrimage was in 1949 and I was nearly seven years of age. It was in March, just before Easter. There were few if any men on this pilgrimage and the women seemed to all come from our end of town. All the carriages were full and this was an express train to Ennis, or so Gerry Mahoney thought. The train was to leave at 7 a.m. so before this time, we all went to the station laden with flasks and sandwiches. There was enough to feed an army, for there were no restaurant cars on the West Clare Railway and no toilets either.

Now, who ever thought of this means of transport must have hated pilgrimages because it was a ludicrous way to get to Knock. Kilrush to Ennis is a mere 20 miles by road and it is about 60 miles by rail. The journey by this little train took hours. Father Flynn led the pilgramage. In our carriage there was Auntie May, Katie, Mary, Mrs. Corbett and an unusually serious Cissie Roughan. Before they got to the shrine of Knock they had to say five Rosaries. Perhaps this is why they went the long way around by train to allow them to fit in all of the Rosaries. The first problem Gerry had was when he stopped in Miltown Malbay to take on some water. It appeared that all the ladies wanted to use the toilet and there was only one in the station. The scene became chaotic and the stationmaster had to open the men's toilet for the ladies to use. Gerry's timetable was now behind time but I took the opportunity to get out of the carriage and away from all the prayers to join Gerry up in the engine. The wind was blowing in from the ocean as it always did and you may think that it was warm with a roaring big fire under the boiler. In fact it was still quite cold. I was wrapped up with a jumper and jacket and could still feel the March winds come through the engine cabin.

When we arrived in Ennis we all disembarked and got onto a very large train, one that made the little West Clare engine look like a toy. We then headed off for the shrine of Knock.

We had left Kilrush at about 7 a.m. in the morning and arrived at Knock Station at about 11:30 a.m. We walk from the station to the church at Knock. The walk from the railway station through the village of Knock was quite scenic. We passed a pond with ducks and a little shop similar to Maude Griffin's. Auntie May gave me some money and I went into the shop and bought some ice cream and sweets. We walked on to the church and all stood outside the main door. It was explained to us that it was above this door "Our Lady" had appeared many years before. I think we were half expecting that she would appear again but that was not to be. This was the sacred shrine to the Blessed Virgin Mary. We entered the small church and it was full to capacity just with the people from Kilrush. We had arrived there to celebrate a special Mass and again say the Rosary. To me it was a very small village with a very small church. Our own St. Senan's Church was like a cathedral and would overwhelm the small, humble and simple church of Knock.

After Mass, we all went back to the station and boarded the train for Ennis. When we arrived in Ennis, Gerry and his train was waiting for us. I once again joined him in the engine and escaped from solemn prayers and Rosaries.

All of this has gone in this new era of religion—or has God changed? If so, he has changed dramatically in fifty years. It seems that He doesn't rule by the book of regulations anymore. It seems that He is no longer a vengeful, fearful God. Maybe God has gotten older and more temperate in his ways because today's God seems to want to love people and understand them.

I think I miss some of the harshness of the old God and his Church in the days gone by because the retreat, with all its fear and frightening methods was, in a way, a means of entertainment and it took a lot of the boredom out of our lives. We had something to talk about that was different. You would hear the saying, "Don't go to that priest. He is an Almighty man and he will give you an awful penance." The women would sit around the fire and talk about what the priests had told them. Half the time they would be serious but there would be an awful lot of laughter as they appreciated the lighter side of what was said in the sermons. To us, as simple people, we would certainly believe everything they said. It would not be hard to believe that the devil actually lived down the road, because he was very real to us.

So God has changed to blend in with this new technological world. He has his own radio and television stations. He has a web site and you can converse over the Internet with Him. People can even go to mass in there own living room; they don't need the church anymore. Today's preachers are a different kind of individual, a different kind of person as they preach the love of God and the love of your fellow man. They preach about the kindness and the goodness of God. Yet despite the understanding of this new God, I sometimes miss the old days with the old God and his book of regulations, the voice of thunder and the terrible punishments.

CHAPTER TWENTY EIGHT

Fair Day in Kilrush

Horse Fairs have always been a tradition in Ireland. It is at the horse fair that everybody who had an interest in horses or donkeys could meet and trade. Livestock breeders, horse dealers, farmers, racing enthusiasts, in fact anybody who were needing to buy or sell horses or donkeys would be rubbing shoulders with each other. Be it a thoroughbred for racing or a draught horse for ploughing, bargaining over the price was long, loud and hard. The fair would be attended by many who had no intention of indulging in trade, but rather to meet up with old friends or make new ones. It was an occasion enjoyed by all.

Of course, when it comes to breeding quality horses, Ireland has no match. Those great men of European history, the Duke of Wellington and Napoleon faced each other at Waterloo both with legs astride Irish horses. Wellington rode an Irish black named Copenhagen purchased for him at the fair in Cahirmee, County Cork while Napoleon's mount Marengo had been bred in Kilmuckridge, Co. Wexford.

It was not just horses for military use the Irish had became famous, but also what is known as "The Sport of Kings," horse racing. Many famous Irish-bred horses have been led into the winner's circle in such racing classics as the British Grand National, held annually at Aintree, near

Liverpool and both the English and Kentucky Derby's.

There is not a race of people in the world who knows and understands horses like the Irish. For centuries the horse has been the backbone of its economy, the engine that powered its agricultural endeavours.

When the cups are full, many an argument is waged in the bars of Ireland as to just who, out of an almost endless list, was the finest thoroughbred horse ever. Usually it will come down to two names, Arkle and Boomerang. Arkle was a mighty horse, but Boomerang is on record as having won four consecutive Hickstead Derbys, the horse trials at Badminton, recognised as one of the toughest courses in the world.

For some unknown reason, the Kilrush Fair was acknowledged as one of the most important, and therefore one of the biggest in Ireland, sharing that title with Ballinasloe.

There would be literally hundreds of animals from asses, donkeys, ponies, hunters, workhorses and shires. The quality of many animals could not be bettered anywhere else in the world. Buyers and sellers would come from all over Ireland and England for this spectacular day. Fair Day would find horses all the way along Henry St. down to the Square into Frances St. and along Moore St. There would be horses as far as the eye could see.

The fair day happened about twice a year and it was really good for two reasons. One was that the Fair Day was always a holiday for school children and secondly we could make money, well at least I could, because I could and would ride any horse you gave me.

Senan and Paddy just considered it a day off school. However if you used your head and watched the farmers coming in you could pick a farmer with a string of good horses. Prices ranged from a pound for a donkey up to thirty pounds for a top horse.

On fair day, I would get to Henry Street at about eight o'clock in the morning. I would look for a farmer with at least one handy looking horse. This particular day I was outside Kelly's bar on the corner of Henry and Vandeleur Streets and my usual line when I found the right man and the right horses was to ask if I could mind his horses.

Fully knowing the game, the farmer would ask, "Can you ride?"

"Yes sir," I could answer. "I'm good at it."

"We'll soon find out about that," he would answer. "A couple of my horses are a bit skitty."

"That's alright, sir," I would answer. "I can handle them."

"What's your name, son?" he asked.

"Joe, sir," I answered.

"Okay, Joe," he said. "This sorrel here is a bit frigit. Can we fix her up before the buyers arrive?"

"Yes, sir," I confidently answered. "I'll take her up the Kilkee Road a couple of times and that should keep her quiet."

As the farmer well knew, the Kilkee Road was a long, steep hill as it left Kilrush.

He smiled. "That's a good lad, give her good run but watch her," he said.

"She'll be fine, sir," I answered.

"Will you be wanting a saddle?" he asked.

"No, sir," I replied. "I can't ride if I have a saddle."

"You're a real rider then," commented the farmer. "Ride a horse with your arse as you should do. Good lad."

The sorrel was about fifteen hands high and a beautiful horse. She was a nicely coloured chestnut with a white a blaze on her head and flaxen main and tail. She was high spirited and about 3 years old. In time she would be a really good riding horse. This was the type of horse a well to do man would buy for his daughter and because of its looks, it would usually be a bit more expensive that the normal pony.

This was a fine boned pony with a good head; there was a little bit of Arab in her somewhere. She had that proud head and carried herself well. I thought it should not be hard to sell this pony.

As far as the farmers were concerned this was a day out for them and they spent all day in the bars. It was one of those big social occasions for the local farmers and they came from miles around. They would haggle about a horse, get to the luck and walk away cursing and swearing. It would not be a Fair Day without a couple of fights somewhere on the streets. This was standard and kept Guard Gildea busy for a while in what is normally a sleepy town out in the west of Clare. The Garda would send reinforcements from one of the local towns for the day. There were always a lot of gypsies in town on Fair Day and they had a good eye for a horse.

The farmer I had met had three other horses besides the sorrel. She was acting up though.

"I think she needs a hard run," I said.

"I'm sure she does," agreed the farmer.

He held on to the other three horses with one hand and gave me a leg up on the sorrel with the other. Her movements were unsettling the other horses. I could see the farmer eyeing me, trying to judge if I could handle her.

I got on her back and I could feel her move and she really was agitated, throwing her head up and moving all over the place. I was about 40 yards from the bottom of the Kilkee Road and I just let her go. She took off at a full gallop. I just sat there and encouraged her. I knew that there was not a horse on this planet that could run all the way up the Kilkee Road hill. I knew it but the horse did not. By the time she reached the turn off for the creamery, only about 200 yards up, she was done in. She had had enough but I pushed her on further to quiet her down. Within another 150 yards of kicking her on and pushing her she was really finished and a lather of sweat. She was sweating more from winding herself up with excitement than the run, and I felt that she would need a few more times up and down the hill before she would really settle. This was a young horse that was a bit green and needed to be ridden by an experienced rider. It was definitely not a horse for a beginner.

I brought her down and she knew she'd had a run and very quietly came down the hill. She turned a few heads though when I stopped at the water pump on the corner of the schoolhouse at the cross. By the time I had wiped her down with a cloth she looked really good but very tired.

As I returned to the pub, the farmer was smiling, the delight on his face plain to see. "Well done Joe," he said. "You have done this before?"

"Yes, sir," I replied. "Many times."

"Okay, Joe," the farmer said. "Look after the horses and I'll be in the bar if you need me."

He turned and went back into Kelly's bar; confident I knew horses and wouldn't let a potential buyer go by. Once someone was seriously looking at one of the horses, I would call him out and he would haggle a price. By midday we had sold a grey mare for ten pounds and a solid looking carthorse for seventeen pounds.

Come the afternoon and the sorrel was still unsold. I had to take her up the hill a couple of more times before she got the message not to run like hell. We eventually sold her to a farmer and the haggling was hard.

The customer wanted to see her move so I hopped on her back and she did not move. She was so frightened that I would take her up the hill again. She was quiet and well behaved, although mind you, she had nothing left in her. The farmer was impressed that he was getting a quiet horse and asked if his daughter could ride her.

We put a saddle on and she was a perfect lady and walked and trotted up and down the street. Now everyone was happy and the customer started the bid.

"What do want for the horse?" he asked.

"I'll take thirty-five pounds, and not a penny less," said the farmer.

"Will you fok off and go away our that. That's an awful fokking price you're asking," replied the customer. "I'll give you fifteen, and you should be grateful."

Ten minutes furious bargaining, and a price of twenty-five pounds was agreed, but fiercer bargaining was yet to take place over the "Good Luck."

It was a firm tradition in that part of Ireland that the seller would return a small part of the purchase price to the buyer as "good luck." Before the money was handed over, each would spit on their own hand then the palms would be slapped together to seal the deal.

The customer was obviously looking for a pound back for "good luck." This, as far as my man was concerned, was just too much. The many pints of porter swilling around inside of him made him stubborn. The best he would offer was five shillings. Much spitting on the hands took place as each expected to other to cave in and slap palms together to seal the deal. So much were they shouting that an interested crowd gathered, and one man decided he would try to be the middleman, as it was always rewarded with a pint or two of porter. The middleman was a big man, about 6 feet tall, 50 years of age with a flat cap on the side of his head wearing a big black overcoat and Wellington boots. He had enjoyed a few jars already and had froth in the corner of his mouth as he spoke.

"For foks sake man, will you give me the fokking luck?" asked the customer.

"Give the man the luck and be off," suggested the middleman.

"You have five shillings," shouted the farmer. "Sure man, what the fok do you want?"

"For foks sake, man, give me a pound for the luck and let's away home," shouted the customer.

"Will you fokking meet him halfway?" The middleman asked the farmer.

"Fok off. I will not," shouted the farmer. "He has the five, let him be off."

"Fok this is too hard. Away wid you man," said the customer, realizing he was getting no where. "For foks sake, will you meet me half way?"

Still the farmer refused. Then the middleman came up with a compromise.

"Now my boyyos, and by the twenty-four balls of the twelve apostles," said the middleman. "This is the final deal. We don't want your daughter upset for a few fokking bob, do we?"

"No," said the customer.

"Let's go to ten bob for foks sake and your man their will buy the porter," said the middleman. "Is it a deal?"

Reluctantly they agreed, spat on their hands and gave a big slap. The deal was sealed and the farmer's daughter was holding the horse as they walked into Doyle's Bar for the porter.

As I handed over the horse, I thought, "I would hate to ride her without a hill close by in the morning."

The farmer came up to me smiling. The normal price that you got paid on a Fair Day was about half a crown. "Joe," he said. "There is five shillings for a good day's work and here is another ten bob."

I was delighted but shocked.

"I would not give him the pound good luck," continued the farmer. "But whatever I saved was yours. So here you are boy. You did a good job with that sorrel," he went on. "Without that I don't think we would have got as much for her or even sold her." He handed over the fifteen shillings. "Well done, boyyo. You did a great job today."

He put his hand on my head and tussled my hair. "Come on Joe let's have a drink. Tie that horse up there."

I tied the remaining horse to the post and we went into Doyle's pub where he bought me a drink of orange and some Smiths Crisps. Mr. and Mrs. Doyle were behind the bar being very busy.

I left the farmer in Doyle's Bar with the remaining horse still tied up out the front. The farmer was more than happy and so was I.

Well I went of home and was very proud of my day and my fifteen shillings, which was a fortune in those days.

CHAPTER TWENTY NINE

Our Motor Boat

S ean used to work as the engineer on the Dingle. The Dingle was a small 200 ton coaster that travelled between Kilrush and Limerick. It belonged to Glynn's Flourmills and transported the flour up the river and returned with general goods for the town. The other boat of Glynn's was called the Alita, which was skippered by Mattie Carroll. Ryan's flourmill had a smaller wooden trader boat of about 120 tons called the St. Senan. These three little traders The Dingle, the Alita and the St. Senan carried a lot of goods to the town in the late forties and fifties. They sometimes delivered flour to the other towns such as Tarbert.

Sean bought a clinker built lifeboat from a ship that was being scrapped in Limerick. The boat was 32 foot long, a big and heavy boat for oars. The boat was brought back to Kilrush on the deck of the Dingle, unloaded at the boathouse before going into The Creek and then rowed over to Glynn's warehouse on the dock. We left the boat on the grass just by the edge of the slipway.

The boys decided that this could be turned into a good motorboat, so a new project began. They bought an old Austin Seven car that looked to be very beat up, so was very cheap. They weren't interested in the body, just the engine. Amid much laughter, the car was driven to the boathouse and they began to dismantle it bit by bit. Andrew was at home during this project and as he was an aircraft engineer in the RAF he was also recruited.

They first removed the engine, gearbox and shaft out of the car and fixed the lot into the boat. The clutch was worked from a handle that was pulled up whilst engaging the gears. Sean put a fifteen-inch propeller on the shaft because it was the only one they could get. It was designed to drive far bigger boats but then, beggars can't be choosers.

The boat was brought over to the warehouse and put on the dock wall. Sean and Andrew had to do some work on the shaft and prop before putting it into the water. Eventually the boat was launched without a great deal of ceremony. The original shaft from the motorcar had been used with no added extension. The Austin Seven was not a very long car. This meant that the engine had to be mounted quite near the stern. The first thing that happened when we launched the boat into the water was the bow came up too high. Hauling two large, solid-concrete blocks to the boat and placing them in the bow solved this problem, although the boat was now a lot lower in the water than before.

It was high tide so we decided to give it a test run. Gerard, who was working that afternoon in the mill, was watching us from the window. There being no battery, the engine was started by using the crank handle. Amazingly, the engine fired up and ran like a dream. Once we were all aboard, Sean lifted the handle on the clutch and put it into first gear. The boat slowly moved forward and Sean gave it a few more revs. We left the dock, turned past the Customs House, the old sailing ship wreck, past the quay and on out to the boathouse. When we got to the boathouse it was decided to put the engine into second gear. This had the effect of powering the boat so fast that the bow came up again and we were taking water over the stern. Although it was a bit frightening everyone was laughing. Deciding that the first gear was ample, Sean changed down and off we went for a trip. Our maiden voyage took us out past Cappagh to the end of Hog Island. We then came up the lea side of Hog and back between Scattery and Hog and across back into The Creek. We were well satisfied with the boat and how she handled. The boat was to give us years of excellent service as well as be a lot of fun.

CHAPTER THIRTY

The Winds Of Change

So the years of my childhood advanced. It was a seemingly endless road where the responsibilities of adulthood had yet to appear above the horizon. Although there were changes in the life of Kilrush, they came so gradually as to be almost unnoticed. Virtually ever house became electrified. Frances Street witnessed an increase in motor vehicles every year. The radio was enjoyed as evening entertainment, but for most part, life went on at its leisurely pace, geared to the seasons. There were the usual marriages, funerals, births and Church celebrations. There was the odd party to say farewell to yet another of the youth of Kilrush as they abandoned the hope of local employment and left to seek their fortunes elsewhere. In spite of electricity, the turf still had to be brought in every summer, stacked or sold. Summer evenings still drew Sean and me to the river to catch trout. Weekdays were the time for school and its tortures and terrors. What had been Katie's babies became people to play with and adore. Auntie May was always there, baking her bread or enjoying her tay. Between doing my chores, fishing, scouting with Willie, playing football and hanging around with my friend Senan, life was always full. It couldn't last. When ever life gets too good, God sometimes has a way to balance it with a bit of suffering.

My thundercloud came in May 1957, when I was not yet fifteen years of age. It was one of those wonderful spring afternoons. The southwest wind brought the clouds rolling in over the Kerry Mountains. The sun on them produced a wonderful kaleidoscope of pinks and greys.

I was walking home from school with Senan and Pat O'Brien. We were all joking as we walked, happy that we were on our way home. We were passing Sue Morrissey's house and she was at the door.

"Hello there, Sue," I said.

"Faiten, Joe," she replied in her usual cheerful way. "It's a grand day altogether."

"Where's Jack?" I inquired. "With the hounds I suppose."

"Where else, he's hound mad, as you well know," she replied. "I think you'll be having visitors at home, Joe."

At this, I glanced across the road to our house. Nothing looked different. We stopped at Senan's gate, chatted some more, said our good-byes and I sauntered over to our house, opened the gate and as I turned to close it, my mother came running down the path with open arms and crying. I had no idea what to do. I was stunned and shocked. I had not seen my mother for five years and here she was with her arms around me kissing me. I was speechless.

She was all excited and took me into the house telling me how much I had grown. Mother was talking to me all the time but I had no idea what it was she was saying. We walked along the hall and into the kitchen. There I received a bigger, although not necessary a nicer surprise. My father was sat down behind the door. I didn't know it then, but my whole life had been ripped asunder in that short walk from gate to kitchen. The idyllic world that I lived in had just been shaken to its roots.

My father stood up and shook my hand and I had

another quick thought. "What the hell do I call him?" The last time I had seen him I had been just four years old, nearly eleven years previous.

My father looked different than I had imagined. He was the same height as me, the same colour hair and he was smartly dressed in a suit and tie with highly polished shoes.

"Hello, son," he said with a smile.

I took a chance on the mode of address and replied, "Hello, dad."

He smiled again and sat down. He was cold compared to Sean and the lads as they would have put their arm around my shoulder and given me a squeeze. This was nothing like that; it was a very clinical first meeting

"How are things in school?" he asked.

"Fine," I replied.

This was becoming a very strained conversation; the talk did not flow at all. He had difficulty in conversing with a young lad with a very strong Irish accent and to me he sounded like one of those people in the films. In fact he may as well have been in the films. I could not come to terms with the situation because I still held real fears concerning my father. I did not have any good memories of him as a small boy.

My parents stayed about five days in all and I really cannot remember what we did or what was said in all those days they were in Kilrush.

My father did everything the boys did not do. He went to the pub every afternoon and night. The afternoons were spent in Frank MacCauliff's bar and nights at Mrs. Crotty's whom he knew very well. When he had lived in Kilrush he was well know for his piano playing. He would play the piano in Mrs. Crotty's pub while she would accompany him on her concertina. My father had played at the dances in the Town Hall and most people knew who he was.

The boys, of course, never had a drink except at

Christmas and then probably only one glass of sherry. Sean was the only one that smoked.

My father and I hardly spoke at all. We did not speak about anything meaningful except to say good morning and then I would not see him or my mother to say goodnight.

The reason for their visit was that my father had arrived back from South America and they needed a few days holiday. They decided to toss a coin. If it was heads they would go to Blackpool and if tails they would come and see me. The outcome of course was they came to see me. One could say I lost the toss and with it, my way of life.

My father decided that I needed to go back to England for a holiday to see my brothers and sisters. He made the arrangements and we were to fly from Shannon Airport. Gerald Griffin was hired for the day and took us to the airport while Auntie May and Willie came with us. I was dressed in my usual jacket and short trousers, knee length socks and highly polished shoes, thanks to Willie's efforts.

"Riley. Don't be getting into any trouble over there," said Willie

"What sort of trouble?" I asked.

"You leave them English girls alone," he said with a smile and a wink.

We sat in the bar and my father and mother had a drink while Auntie May and Willie had a cup of tea.

My father took out his cheque book and wrote out a check for 100 pounds and gave it to Auntie May.

Auntie May smiled as she took the check. She had never seen that much money at once. I was speechless and ashamed. My father playing the big "I Am", putting the value of her keeping me in Kilrush for eleven years at less than ten pounds a year. I have and never will forgive or forget this. My Auntie May had clothed me, fed me and loved me for eleven years. My father, even though he must have always been earning good money, never once sent any to her towards my keep. It was not just the amount of money; it was the arrogance of his flourish as he handed the check that made me angry. He expected Auntie May to be grateful and think well of him for this gesture, and Auntie May, being the angel she was, complied. Willie looked at me and could see my anger. I was lost for words.

Auntie May was crying and I knelt down in front of her and it was my turn to console her.

"I will be back in a week, Auntie May," I said. "Don't cry."

"It will be all right, boy," she said, putting her hands on my face. I was now in tears. I kissed Auntie May good-bye and Willie gave me a big hug. With a tear in his eye, he said, "Get back here soon, boyyo. Don't forget to go to Mass on Sunday."

We walked out to the plane. It was a DC3 Aer Lingus flight to Dublin, where we would catch another one for Manchester. The plane had two seats on either side of the aisle. I sat on my own and my mother and father sat behind me. I had never been on a plane before and it was exciting, but my emotions were torn. My father in his usual arrogant way had demanded that I go back to England for a holiday. I had no say in the matter and neither did anyone else in Kilrush.

CHAPTER THIRTY ONE

Pain And Confusion

A s the plane landed at Manchester Airport a great depression came over me. Here I was about to enter the land of my birth where I was a complete stranger. From the airport, we took a taxi to the railway station. We eventually arrived in Thornaby about eight o'clock that night.

As we walked up the path to the house, memories flooded back about my previous unhappy visit and I was to discover I had good reason to believe that this one would not prove any better.

The ridicule started almost as soon as I entered the house. Back in Kilrush, virtually every boy of my age was still dressed in short pants. This was not the case in England where boys wore long trousers from the age of twelve. To my brothers, and later all the kids around the neighbourhood, the sight of me, a boy the same height as his father, wearing short pants was the cause for much hilarity and insults. Communication was so difficult that I could well have been in France or Germany. I had great difficulty in understanding their thick Geordie dialect although they had a more difficult time in understanding me talking rapidly with a west Clare accent.

Even the family would admonish me. "Stop, Joe," one

would say. "I can't understand a word you're saying. Start again, will you?" This happened so often that it became embarrassing. I didn't know if they were telling the truth or just ribbing me because of my way of talking.

My mother quickly overcame the embarrassment of my short pants by going to Stockton and returning with a pair of long pants for me. I just wished that she had been able to purchase a Geordie accent as well.

I do not remember much of my stay in Thornaby. I met my younger sisters Judith and Kathleen for the first time. They were only toddlers and very shy of me.

The only pleasant thing about my stay was that I met a young girl who was the same age as me. Her name was Brenda. She had natural long blonde hair that set off her blue eyes. She was a little tubby but a very pretty girl none-the-less. She made my stay bearable. I spent most of my time with her. She was full of life and we laughed a lot. She understood my Irish accent and that to me was another plus.

Brenda lived next door to Auntie Elsie, an aunt who showed me a great deal of kindness. We would stand at Brenda's front gate and talk until her mother called her indoors at about 10 p.m. I took Brenda to the local pictures and sat in the back row, but it was all very innocent.

When the time thankfully came for me to return home to Kilrush I felt greatly relieved. This time I was old enough to look after myself and did not need envelopes in my pockets. I got on the train at Thornaby together with David and Keith. They travelled with me as far as Darlington, as they were going to do some train spotting there.

I said my good byes to them and headed off for Kilrush with very mixed feelings.

By the following day I had arrived at Limerick at 1:30 in the afternoon and sure enough, there was Gerald Griffin waiting for whoever turned up on boat train.

"Riley. You're back," he said. "And how was Blighty?" (The local slang for England).

"It's okay," I answered. "But I'm glad to be home."

"Not many here today Joe," Gerald observed.

We both stood there for a while until it became obvious that I was going to be the only passenger.

"Okay, Riley," said Gerald. "Let's get going. Your Auntie May will be waiting for you."

Gerald and I talked in general on the winding road from Limerick to Ennis and the bumpy road from Ennis to Kilrush. We came up to the golf course and there the town lay out before me, but this time it was different. It looked the same and I had no idea why it was different.

I got home and Auntie May was at the door waiting for me. I was tired after the long haul and an overnight journey with very little sleep on a hard bench plus a train journey that took forever from Dublin to Limerick.

Willie and the lads were home and as always were interested in what I did and what I had been doing.

That summer seemed to last forever and I became very restless within myself. Everything was the same but somehow I saw it was all so different. I could not settle in any way. I thought about my blood family in England. My mother there would always be my real mother. Nothing on earth could change that fact. My brothers had given me a hard time, but that did not alter the fact that they were my real brothers, sharing the same mother and father. Although I regarded Mary, Katie and Lulu as sisters, my real sisters were over there, in England, where I was born.

But what about my family here, where I was raised? I loved my Auntie May with all of my heart. She was the kindest, most wonderful person in the whole world. She meant everything to me. How about Sean, who I still shared a bed with? Had he not been more to me then any brother could ever have been? There was Gerard and Willie, the finest companions in life anybody could wish for. Did I really belong in this wonderful house or was I just like a cuckoo, borrowing a warm nest for my own ends? I had an Irish name, I spoke with a strong Irish accent, an Irish family had raised me in Ireland, I was now a good Irish Catholic, but the truth was, I would never qualify for an Eire passport.

I was being torn apart inside looking for answers. Every answer just seemed to raise yet another question. The questions in my head, the turmoil of answers were torment, what was I to do? Where did I belong? Just who really was Joe Riley? I cursed the day my father had returned to Kilrush. Prior to his coming, I had never found cause to question my life. These problems, which I felt I could not share with anyone, burned my very soul until I slowly became quiet and withdrawn.

I continued to attend school but my heart was not there. Gerard and I went on the motor bike but I was miles away in my mind. Sean and I went fly-fishing but there was no real interest in me. Going out on the boat was something I had to do and footing the turf from the bog became just a drag. Life was not like it used to be and deep down, I knew it never would be again. I felt I was now on my own and I had no way of knowing how to deal with the situation.

CHAPTER THIRTY TWO

The Wailing Wall

I n late July, as was our usual habit on a Sunday afternoon, I went for a walk. It was usual for a small group of us to walk together either out to Cappagh or to Shanakyle. That particular Sunday, I was in no mood for company, so I went by myself to Cappagh.

My thoughts were in turmoil as I tried to figure out what I should do about my life. I knew that whatever I did, I would be hurting someone who loved me, but nobody could understand the pain I was feeling.

Although the walk along Cappagh was generally invigorating, the wind from the sea removing the cobwebs from the brain, there was one unpleasant stretch and that was passing Doherty's Sawmill. Here, the smell of rotting sawdust was unpleasant to say the least. On that Sunday, so deep was I in thought that I didn't even notice I had passed it.

I returned from my walk in time for tea, and after, I informed Auntie May that I was going to Benediction. The time was just after quarter past seven. I left the house, walked down the path and up the road past the handball alley towards the church. When I left the house I had no other intention than to go to church but something snapped inside of me in those few hundred yards along the way.

I cannot explain what happened to me. I cannot explain

the events that occurred from there on. There is no reasonable or logical explanation as to why instead of turning off to the church, I just kept walking. I walked past the Convent, past Jack O'Deas field, and up to the cross at Henry Street. I still just kept walking, past Reidy's Garage, past Paddy Mescall's forge and on out the Ennis Road. I got to Mike Melican's house at the golf course and chatted for a while at his front door with his mother, Mrs. Melican. She invited me in with the usual welcome.

"Joe," she asked. "Will you have a sup of tay?"

I must have hesitated and looked a little distracted, for she then said, "Joe. Are you alright?"

I snapped out of my thoughts. "Yes, Ma'am," I said. "Thank you, Ma'am. I will have a sup of tay if it's all right." I entered the thatched cottage, smelled the turf fire and said "God bless all here."

I had a cup of tea and we passed the time talking about the weather and school. I said good bye to Mike and his mother and walked up the hill of the Ennis Road.

I crossed over the road at the top of the hill and sat on the wall. The evening was now drawing in and I sat there for the next half an hour. So many things were going through my mind about Ireland and England and my two families.

I looked down on the town; the spire of St. Senan's Church, the flourmills and The Creek. I looked out over the Shannon estuary, at the island's of Hog and Scattery where I had played so much, the Kerry Mountains way in the distance and the woods to the east of the town. This was my world, my town, my playground and my life as a child.

I just sat on that old stone wall and I cried like I had never cried in my life. All of those years of not crying suddenly emerged and welled up inside of me. The surge and the pain inside me were unbearable. I just stayed there on the wall with the tears flooding down my face with all the pain and just wept.

I left Kilrush that night. I took the first step on a journey that was to last nearly 45 years, a journey to find out who was Joe Riley? I looked back on my beloved town and knew in my heart that I would not see it again for many years to come. As Uncle Andrew had taught me, I had to have a plan. As I walked up that road, I knew I had part of that plan. I knew from where I had started, I knew roughly where I wanted to go to, I just hadn't figured how to get there.

Chapter Thirty Three

Victory Savoured

This book has been guided all the way by many spirits and I had no idea of that until today. I had intended the previous chapter to be the last, but after I thought I had finished, I awoke this morning discovering the cross that I had carried all my life had been miraculously lifted from my shoulder. I realized that this book had been guided and blessed by the people whose stories I have told. The ghosts of Kilrush have taken me through my journey that once was a torment and left me with beauty and peace. I am privileged that my ghosts have allowed me to walk with them, to share their lives and at the same time come to terms with my own insecurities so that I am now a happier individual in myself.

It has allowed me to find answers to questions that I had never asked until much later in life. I am sure that psychologists and psychiatrists would have explanations and theories, all of which would mean nothing to me.

I woke up this morning and the tears were tears of joy. For, at last, the hurt, the pain and anger were gone. I could not stop crying or weeping, for today I found myself at last, and my happiness and tears were for the burden I had just laid down. I had faced my wall of fire, walked through to be cleansed and waiting for me and to celebrate with me were all those beautiful people that I met in my childhood.

Writing this book has made me face the ghosts of my past. I have had to face the fact that my parents virtually abandoned me as a young child and the questions that resulted from that. Why me? Why not one of my brothers or sisters? It is this question that haunted me all my life until now and without me realizing it. Raising the ghosts of Kilrush by writing this book allowed me to discover the reason and, better still, be proud of it.

The first realization is; I can choose my friends but I cannot choose my relatives. Now I know the reason as to why my father took me with him in the first place, even more as to why my mother let him.

My mother could be excused somewhat, as in those days in England, the man of the house was king and my father was definitely the king in our household. As far as society was concerned then, wives had no rights. They went along with their husband and stood by him. This was the case in my house. My father was a pitiful man, yet my mother deferred to him all the time, treated him like a king, yet my mother had more brains in her little finger than my father had in his ass.

I will reveal to you what suddenly, in my sleep, came to me. As a child I had become a threat in my own household. My mother loved me too much, treating me as king of the house instead of her husband. He was a very jealous person.

My father was a regular drinker. He would not miss a day without spending his evenings in the pub—never, ever with his family. He would also, on days off, drink during the lunchtime sessions. I never heard a bad word ever said about my father by the men who drank with him. He was the greatest bloke ever, a great mate, always ready with a joke, a smile and the offer of a pint.

At weekends, give him an opportunity to organise or entertain, he was the first called and almost had a fan club.

He was entertaining, was well-versed in matters of the world and smiled all the time. The smile left his face, however, as soon as he passed over the threshold of home. Then he would verbally or even physically attack any member of his family who happened to be in his vicinity.

Why was he like this? He was like this because he was totally immature. He was a little king in his house as a boy and was thoroughly spoiled by his mother. He was then thrust into the real world with a wife and children, yet he was always frightened; frightened of failure, frightened of responsibility. My father was a coward and a bully. He coped with his own fear by making others around him experience more fear than he felt. My father suffered all of his life from insecurity.

To teach my mother a lesson for loving me more than she appeared to love him, he removed me from her, and when he returned without me, he no longer had a rival for her affection. This would also account for the way she then treated my brothers and sisters, almost neglecting their welfare in order not to upset my father again. She loved me, but too much for my father to take. Writing this book has revealed this to me somewhere in my subconscious, and the fact that I didn't see it when I had the opportunity to love her back in later years, as I should have done, makes me feel sad. When my father was too old to intervene, had I understood then, I could have let her know. My mother loved me more than she loved her husband. I can now be proud of that and forgive my father and my anger with life has left me forever. It may be a little late mother, but you have won in the end. Now I understand the pain you must also have felt. Now I truly love you too.

My tears are now tears of joy. They are no longer tears of hurt or pain of a loss I thought I had, but for the beauty of a childhood that very few would experience. I only ever thought of my childhood as being abandoned with lots of questions that matter no more, like poor me and why was I given away at such a young age now mean nothing anymore. What does matter are the people that I was so lucky to be with and how blessed I was to be with them in a great era.

To Paddy Griffin, may God bless you and He needs a good storyteller like you up there. After all someone has to entertain the angels and who better than you Paddy. John Joe O'Shea...I can see you out there John Joe marching out in the front because they will have parades up there for you and maybe you can join God's council.

Jack Hanrahan. I am sure that God has a good batty pony for you with a great cart. Jack, keep a seat for me so that we can once again go out to Cappagh and yak and yarn along the way.

To my family who live in my heart and I have carried around all these years, to my beautiful Auntie May, who loved me all of her life, unselfishly you gave everything and asked for nothing in return. I know that God has you in a special place.

Uncle Andrew. We will make that sail boat again and we will fish the rivers and lakes like we used to and I think that God will give us both a bike and this time I can ride alongside you, and be proud of you as you were of me.

Gerard, Sean, Willie, Johnny, Birdie, Katie, Mary and Lulu "My Ghosts of Kilrush" I love you all and I now lay you down to rest for I now have found peace and can rest with my memories. The Ghosts of Kilrush will live again, as they deserve to, through this book.

You see Uncle Andrew, I believed in my plan and you were right—it worked.

God Bless you all.

Joe Riley
Manila, Philippines.

Ghosts of Kilrush was designed by Tom Suzuki, Tom Suzuki, Inc.,
Fairfax, Virginia. The cover design is also by Tom Suzuki.
The book was printed by Lightning Source U.K., Ltd., Norfolk, U.K.
Cover photo of St. Senan's Well by Patrick Cusack
The text is 11 on 13 Caslon, the display type is Apple Chancery

Printed in the United States
1326500001B/130-150

9 781928 928133